Design History

Following World War I, there was an international attempt to limit re-armament and thus avoid any potential future naval arms race. At first, negotiations focussed on capital ships and discussed limits on gun calibre, displacement and minimum age before replacement. As a result, competition among the major navies was transferred to cruisers and countries immediately started building ships of the maximum size permitted, 10,000 tons standard. The Royal Navy produced the very successful 'County' class (ShipCraft 19), a group of thirteen vessels. Irrespective of any treaty limitations on numbers, however, Great Britain soon realised that it could not afford to keep building such large vessels if they were to be able to produce the number of cruisers deemed necessary. It was also felt that such large cruisers were not ideal for fleet work, and smaller, more manoeuvrable vessels would be preferable.

Persuading other powers to accept smaller cruisers was not easy, but eventually the London Treaty of 1930 defined two different types, 'heavy' cruisers with guns larger than 6.1in and 'light' cruisers with guns smaller than 6.1in. The total tonnage for each type was also agreed; in the case of Great Britain it was 146,800 tons for 'heavy' cruisers and 192,200 tons for 'light' cruisers. The immediate outcome was a class of five vessels with a distinctive appearance – the only single-funnelled cruisers to be built for the Royal Navy since the 1880s – the *Leander* class.

LEANDER CLASS

With a length between perpendiculars (lbp) of 522ft (554ft 3in loa) and a beam of 55ft 8in (*Leander* was 55ft 2in), the ships carried eight 6in/50cal BL Mark XXIII guns in twin Mark XXI mountings, with a maximum elevation of 60°. The standard displacement for the five vessels varied between 6985 and 7270 tons. The quadruple shaft machinery system consisted of four Parsons geared turbines and six Admiralty 3-drum boilers, and produced a nominal 72,000shp giving a nominal top speed of 32.5kts.

Anti-aircraft armament was limited to four 4in/45cal Mark V guns on Mark III high-angle mountings. They were each fitted with two quadruple launchers for 21in torpedoes Mark IX, and carried a catapult to launch either a Hawker Osprey two-seat fighter-reconnaissance seaplane or a Fairey Seafox light reconnaissance seaplane.

Feasibility studies for these cruisers started in the 1920s, and in 1928, the first Sea Lord instructed that five sketch designs should be produced, some having 6in guns and some 5.5in guns, in single or twin mountings. The Staff quickly rejected the 5.5in guns, and although there was a preference for single open mountings, length

This overhead view of HMS *Leander* taken in July 1937, clearly shows the layout of the numerous boats carried. (*US Naval History and Heritage Command, NH 59836*)

LEANDER CLASS BUILDING DATA

Name	Pendant No	Builder	Laid down	Launched	Completed
Leander	75	Devonport DYd *	08.09.30	24.09.31	24.03.33
Achilles	70	Cammell Laird	11.06.31	01.09.32	06.10.33
Orion	85	Devonport DYd *	26.09.31	24.11.32	18.01.34
Neptune	20	Portsmouth DYd **	24.09.31	31.3.33	23.02.34
Ajax	22	Vickers-Armstrong	07.02.33	01.03.34	12.04.35

* machinery by Vickers Armstrong, Tyne; ** machinery by Parsons

dictated that twin mountings on the centreline would provide more guns, with space for a catapult. Twin mountings could also have power loading, more suitable for firing at high angles of elevation.

The Staff Requirement stipulated immunity for the shell rooms and magazines from 6in shells (*ie* light cruiser fire) between 10,000 and 16,000 yards, and from 4.7in shells (*ie* destroyer fire) beyond 7000 yards. Minimum speed was to be 30.5kts at full load, and endurance 7000nm at 16kts. It was estimated that the minimum acceptable displacement was 6000 tons, and the designs were submitted in January 1929. A conference later that month decided that 6000 tons was too small and accepted that a reduced endurance might be necessary. Design 3 was selected and a revised sketch for a larger vessel submitted in May. Inevitably, the design continued to increase in size, the sketch design in August having a waterline length of 547ft, a beam of 54ft, and a displacement of 7000 tons. Board approval was given to the October submission in December. The estimated speed was 31.5kts and endurance 7000nm at 16kts. The 1929/30 programme included just a single 6in-gunned cruiser, HMS *Leander*. Three more, *Achilles*, *Orion* and *Neptune*, were ordered the next year, and *Ajax* the year after that. The beam of the last four vessels was increased, without increasing the breadth at the deck.

Detailed design resulted in an increase in engine power to 72,000shp, 48,000shp on the outer shafts and 24,000shp on the inner shafts, by increasing boiler pressure from 250 to 300psi and maximum revolutions from 280 to 300rpm. To optimise endurance, the forward turbines could be disconnected from the outer shafts. Welding was used to reduce the weight of the cruisers, the extent increasing with each succeeding vessel.

Concern was expressed regarding the watertight sub-division, particularly in the area of the propulsion machinery. The design was changed to include three boiler rooms, each containing two boilers, and three engine rooms – two turbine rooms and the after room containing turbine gearing only. The boiler rooms were all sited forward of the engine rooms, permitting the uptakes to use a single funnel. This did result in a considerable increase in machinery length of 19ft, but the overall increase was minimised by rearranging the layout of the ends of the cruiser. Beam was increased to maintain stability and the depth was increased slightly to preserve the structural strength.

HMS *Achilles* is shown wearing the 'neutrality stripes' on 'B' and 'X' turrets during the Spanish Civil War. She retains her single 4in gun mounts and the hull plating has not yet been extended. Note, she is carrying a Seagull V or Walrus aircraft. (*Navy News*)

Fairey Seafox serial number K-8571 on the catapult of *Orion*. (*US Naval History and Heritage Command, NH 57588*)

The sides of the machinery spaces were protected by 120lb non-cemented (NC) armour on 40lb D1 quality steel, with 50lb D1 steel overhead and 60lb D1 steel end bulkheads. Magazines received additional protection: 140lb NC armour on their sides, with 80lb NC armour crowns and 100lb NC armour end bulkheads. Other areas were not armoured, but the steering gear was protected by 50lb D1 steel overhead and 60lb D1 steel sides. Other important areas, such as the shell rooms, received 40lb D1 steel protection. The last four ships received 60lb D1 steel protection for the transmitting station and low power switchboard room, instead of 40lb.

Another area of discussion was the aircraft facilities, the original design having a 43ft revolving catapult for light aircraft. The Director of Naval Air Department (DNAD) wanted to be able to carry two aircraft, one preferably in a hangar, and to launch heavier aircraft. The Director of Naval Construction (DNC) vetoed the hangar on space grounds but did agree to a heavier 53ft revolving catapult. This was capable of launching a Fairey IIIF aircraft, and space was allocated on the after deckhouse for the stowage of the lighter Hawker Osprey or Fairey Seafox aircraft, but spare aircraft were never actually carried. The Fairey IIIF proved unsuitable, and, as these lighter planes could be launched by a smaller catapult, the later *Ajax* received a 46ft catapult. *Leander* was initially issued with an Osprey floatplane; *Orion*, *Neptune*

This close-up view of the forward superstructure of *Orion* in 1937 shows the forward twin 4in gun to be missing. The rangefinder and fire control directors are clearly visible on the bridge. Note the hull plating has been extended aft level with the aft face of the funnel. (*US Naval History and Heritage Command, NH 57578*)

and *Ajax* all carried the Seafox aircraft at the beginning of war, *Neptune* having carried out the first shipboard catapult launch of this aircraft, from her Type EIIIH catapult, in March 1937.

Barrage AA fire of the 6in guns was a requirement, as was a High Angle Control System (HACS), the DCT being fitted on the bridge roof. Cost-cutting prevented the fitting of a second director tower aft, limiting the guns to just a single target, unless some operated in local control. However, Controller did agree to the installation of a small, simple, non-revolving control position instead of this aft DCT. Because these decisions were not made until late in the design process, the aft control position was not fitted to *Leander*.

Light AA armament was to be four 0.5in quad machine gun mounts, but the forward two were removed as a cost-saving measure. As the aft HADCT was not fitted, it was decided to fit a third 0.5in quad mount instead. In some of the class, the two mounts abreast the bridge were relocated to the aft superstructure, but concern was expressed, as a single hit could then knock out all three mounts.

Three 36in searchlights were fitted, one on each side of the funnel, and one aft of the mainmast. Two 12ft rangefinders were mounted on the bridge. The class was fitted with Asdic Type 132, and, for self defence, a short depth charge rail was fitted on the port quarter.

Concern was expressed about the standards of accommodation provided, the space per man being less than in the 'County' class cruisers. In order to minimise size, this was accepted. Initial complement was 570, but, due to wartime modifications, particularly the addition of small AA weapons, this increased noticeably, exacerbating the problem of space shortage.

On trials over a measured mile in the Clyde in December 1932, *Leander* achieved a speed of 32.45kts, at a displacement of 7265 tons. At deep load, 9010 tons, the speed was 31.4 knots. *Neptune* carried out her trials on the Talland course in December 1933, achieving 30.79kts at a displacement of 8617 tons; and *Ajax* achieved 33.06kts at 7170 tons on the Arran measured mile in 1935. *Ajax* was the lightest of the class, and was fitted with a different design of propellers to *Leander*.

Each cruiser cost approximately £1,613,000, excluding guns.

In this photograph of *Sydney* taken in 1936, the single 4in gun mounts are clearly visible.

MODIFIED *LEANDER* CLASS

Three vessels were laid down for the Royal Navy to follow on from the *Leander* class. The *Leanders* were felt to be vulnerable to a single torpedo hit disabling the entire propulsion system, and so in these vessels the arrangement of boiler and engine rooms was changed to the 'unit system': boiler room – engine room – boiler room – engine room. They were often referred to as the 'Modified' or 'Improved' *Leander* class, but having been taken over by the Australian Navy soon after completion, they were also referred to as the *Perth* class (the first vessel to be laid down and launched, but the last to be completed) or the *Sydney* class (the first vessel to be completed).

Of similar dimensions to the *Leanders*, and carrying the same armament, the most obvious difference was the two funnels, resulting from the rearrangement of the boiler and engine rooms. The number of boilers was reduced to four in two boiler rooms, but the power generated remained the same. The rearrangement required more length for the machinery spaces, but did reduce weight. The outboard shafts were driven by the forward unit.

They retained the same lbp of 522ft as the *Leander* class, but overall they were just under eight feet longer at 562ft 3in, and had a greater beam of 56ft 8in. Displacement was also similar, varying between 6830 and 7105 tons, standard.

MODIFIED *LEANDER* CLASS BUILDING DATA

Name	Pendant No	Builder	Laid down	Launched	Completed
Perth (ex-*Amphion*)	I29, D29	Portsmouth DYd*	26.06.33	27.07.34	06.07.36
Sydney (ex-*Phaeton*)	I48, D48	Swan Hunter	08.07.33	22.09.34	24.09.35
Hobart (ex-*Apollo*)	I63, D63, C3	Devonport DYd	15.08.33	09.10.34	13.01.36

* machinery by Beardmore

Accommodation was very cramped and the aircraft facilities were limited, as the large 53ft revolving catapult could not be fitted. The 46ft catapult could only launch the two-seater fleet reconnaissance aircraft.

The legend was approved in November 1932, but, during further discussions, the distance between the funnels was increased by six feet, allowing the 53ft catapult to be fitted. Financial restrictions also resulted in changes, including, as in the *Leander* class, the omission of an aft DCT. Consideration was given to the fitting of a fixed, flush athwartships catapult, and the deletion of the crane. Consideration was also given to the fitting of more 6in guns by using triple turrets, but the idea was rejected.

Ten alternative layouts of boats and aircraft facilities were produced, and in January 1934, the Board gave approval for the fitting of the 46ft deck integrated light

A closer photograph of *Sydney*, showing, the single 4in gun mounts in more detail.

Left: This photograph of *Apollo* was taken during a visit to Miami in early 1938 and clearly shows the anchor-handling arrangements on the forecastle. (*US Naval History and Heritage Command, NH 58634*)

Right: The launch of *Arethusa* at Chatham Dockyard on 6 March 1934, the many umbrellas on display in the group of onlookers indicating that it was a rainy day. (*US Naval History and Heritage Command, NH 63159*)

Right: This port bow view of *Penelope*, clearly shows the quadruple 0.5in mounting forward and the twin 4in mountings aft.

Below: A fine profile view of *Hobart* in harbour prior to the war, with awnings protecting deck areas from the heat. (*US Naval History and Heritage Command, NH 60599*)

22
21
20
19
18
17
16
15
14
13
12
11
10

ARETHUSA CLASS BUILDING DATA

Name	Pendant No	Builder	Laid down	Launched	Completed
Arethusa	26, C26	Chatham DYd	25.01.33	06.03.34	23.05.35
Galatea	71, C71	Scotts	02.06.33	09.08.34	14.08.35
Penelope	97, C97	Harland & Wolff	30.05.34	15.10.35	13.11.36
Aurora	12, C12	Portsmouth DYd	23.07.35	20.08.36	12.11.37

type catapult. The agreement to transfer the ships to Australia, who required the larger Seagull or Walrus aircraft, resulted in the fitting of the 53ft revolving catapult.

The AA armament was limited to four single 4in mountings, around the aft funnel, and three quadruple 0.5in mountings, two athwart the bridge and one on the aft superstructure.

ARETHUSA CLASS

This class was very similar to the Modified *Leander* class, but with 'X' turret omitted. They were shorter, with a waterline length of 480ft and a beam of 51ft. As well as one 6in turret less, the number of torpedo tubes was reduced to six, two triple rather than quadruple mountings. They did retain the same 4in AA guns, but these were grouped aft of the second funnel, and only two quadruple 0.5in machine gun mounts were fitted, forward of the fore funnel. The first two, *Arethusa* and *Galatea*, completed with single 4in mountings, but the last two, *Penelope* and *Aurora*, completed with twin mountings. The complement was reduced to 500.

Discussions on this class were started in 1929, and the design decided in early 1931. The Labour government delayed any orders, and so the design was reconsidered again, being finalised in February 1932. Their displacements varied between 5031 and 5458 tons, standard. The unit machinery arrangement was approved for this class before it was adopted for the Modified *Leander* class. A catapult was fitted between the funnels, initially for a Hawker Osprey floatplane, being replaced by a Fairey Seafox after November 1937. Controller wanted to include a second aircraft, and it was eventually agreed that in an emergency an Osprey, with folded wings, could be stowed on the aft deckhouse, between the 4in guns.

The protection of the *Arethusa* class was less than that of the *Leanders*, with 90lb NC armour on the sides, 40lb D1 steel being used. The magazines had 120lb NC armour on the sides, and 80lb NC armour sides and ends.

Each cruiser cost approximately £1,200,000, excluding guns.

This starboard quarter view of *Arethusa* in June 1935, dressed overall, clearly shows the grouping of the 4in AA guns, aft of the funnels.

Wartime Actions and Losses

AJAX AND *ACHILLES* AND THE BATTLE OF THE RIVER PLATE

The first significant naval action of the Second World War occurred on 13 December 1939 and involved the 'B'-type heavy cruiser *Exeter* and two *Leander* class light cruisers, *Ajax* and *Achilles*, taking on the German 'pocket battleship' *Admiral Graf Spee*.

Heavily outgunned, the British split into two groups. *Admiral Graf Spee* opened fire first, concentrating on *Exeter* which soon received a hit on 'B' turret, followed by another on 'A' turret. Her hull was also badly damaged and she developed a list of 7°. However, *Exeter* did achieve a hit on the enemy with her 8in guns, damaging her fuel system.

Ajax and *Achilles* closed the range and scored hits with their 6in guns, causing *Graf Spee* to split her fire. *Ajax* did launch her Fairey Seafox spotter floatplane from her catapult but, at 0725, she received an 11in delayed-action hit on the after superstructure. The shell passed through various cabins, then 'X' turret trunk, wrecking the turret machinery below the gunhouse and finally bursting in the Commodore's sleeping cabin, doing considerable damage. A portion of the base of the shell struck 'Y' barbette close to the training rack and jammed the turret. This shell killed four and wounded six of 'X' turret's crew. This one hit therefore put both 'X' and 'Y' turrets out of action. At 0724 *Ajax* turned to starboard and fired four torpedoes at a range of 9000 yards. By 0738 *Ajax* had only three guns in action, as one of the hoists had failed in 'B' turret. One of *Graf Spee*'s last salvos brought down *Ajax*'s main topmast and destroyed all her aerials. Jury aerials were, however, soon rigged.

Exeter in April 1934. *(US Naval History and Heritage Command, NH 60812)*

Graf Spee anchored in Montevideo after the Battle of the River Plate. Note the camouflage pattern. (*US Naval History and Heritage Command, NH 59658*)

With no repair facilities available nearby, *Graf Spee* made for neutral Montevideo, pursued by the light cruisers. At 0807 *Ajax*'s aerials were still down, and so *Achilles* was ordered to broadcast *Graf Spee*'s position, course and speed to all British merchant ships. A similar message was broadcast every hour from *Ajax* until the end of the chase. At 0912, *Ajax* recovered her aircraft. At 1005 *Achilles*, overestimating the enemy's speed, had closed to 23,000 yards. *Graf Spee* thereupon altered course and fired two three-gun salvos at *Achilles*; the first was very short, but the second fell close alongside.

Achilles suffered four fatalities and *Ajax*, seven. Captain William Edward Parry, RN, of *Achilles*, and Captain Charles Henry Lawrence Woodhouse, RN, of *Ajax*, were both made Companions of the Most Honourable Order of the Bath, and received the DSO. The Conspicuous Gallantry Medal was awarded to Samuel John Trimble, Sergeant, Royal Marines, HMS *Achilles*. The DSC was awarded to six members and the DSM to fourteen members of *Ajax*'s crew. *Achilles*' crew received four DSCs and fourteen DSMs. There were also numerous members of both crews that were Mentioned in Despatches.

Following a British disinformation campaign, Captain Langsdorff decided to scuttle *Graf Spee*.

Graf Spee was scuttled to save further loss of life. (*US Naval History and Heritage Command, NH 51977-A*)

Later *Ajax* was involved in both the Battle of Crete and the Battle of Malta. She was disabled by a 1000lb bomb hitting 'B' boiler room on 1 January 1943 while at Bône. Permanent repairs took place in the United States where she was taken in hand at Norfolk Navy Yard, Virginia. As part of Force 'K', *Ajax* bombarded Gold Beach during the D-Day invasion.

LEANDER AND THE BATTLE OF KOLOMBANGARA

As part of Task Force 36.1, on 12 July 1943, *Leander* took part in the Battle of Kolombangara, when she received a hit from a Japanese 24in torpedo, which knocked out both boiler rooms, repairs taking more than two years.

LOSS OF *NEPTUNE*

Neptune, commanded by Captain Rory O'Conor, was leading Force 'K', a cruiser raiding squadron, their task being to destroy German and Italian convoys carrying troops and supplies to Libya, in support of Rommel's army in North Africa. On the afternoon of 18 December 1941, the squadron was despatched from Malta to intercept an important enemy convoy bound for Tripoli. The three cruisers of Force 'K', *Neptune*, *Aurora* and *Penelope*, supported by the destroyers *Kandahar*, *Lance*, *Lively* and *Havock*, were steaming south, in single line ahead on a dark, stormy night when at 0106, *Neptune* struck a mine. *Aurora*, her next astern, hauled out to starboard but only a minute later she too exploded a mine; two minutes later an explosion buffeted *Penelope*'s port side abreast the bridge. *Neptune*, going full astern, hit another mine, which wrecked her steering gear and propellers and brought her to a standstill.

Leander at anchor in Solomon Islands waters, 25 July 1943, photographed from USS *Nicholas* (DD-449). *(US Naval History and Heritage Command, 80-G-56728)*

Aurora contrived to turn and steam out of the field without further catastrophe, followed by *Penelope*; Captain Agnew, in command of *Aurora*, considered the situation in all its dire gravity. They were 15 miles from Tripoli and it was nearly dawn. The damage to *Aurora* had reduced her maximum speed to 10 knots, and his duty was to get her as far from the enemy coast as he could before daylight. The risk of sending another ship into the minefield to tow *Neptune* out was hardly justified but the need to save life made it imperative. The destroyers *Kandahar* and *Lively* then entered the minefield in an attempt to reach *Neptune* and tow her out. Captain Nicholl was also cautiously edging *Penelope* towards her when at 0318 *Kandahar* struck a mine. Captain O'Conor flashed a warning: 'Keep away'. At 0403 *Neptune* struck a fourth mine which exploded amidships, and she slowly turned over and sank.

With 737 crew members dead, thirty crew members initially survived the sinking but later died, only one being still alive when their carley float was picked up five days later by the Italian torpedo boat

Orion off the Mare Island Navy Yard, California, 20 February 1942. *(US Naval History and Heritage Command, 80-G-170871)*

Generale Achille Papa. The sole survivor, Able Seaman Norman Walton, spent 18 months in an Italian prisoner of war camp.

ORION AND THE BATTLE OF CAPE MATAPAN

At the end of March 1941, *Orion* played an important part in the Battle of Cape Matapan. She was operating as part of Force 'B', under Admiral Sir Henry Pridham-Wippell. Force 'B' also included the light cruisers *Ajax*, *Gloucester* and *Perth*, and the destroyers *Hasty*, *Hereward* and *Ilex*. On 27 March, Force 'B' sailed from Greek waters for a position south of Crete. On the same day, Admiral Cunningham, with three battleships and an aircraft carrier left Alexandria to meet the cruisers.

The cruisers became involved in an action with Italian cruisers and, at one point, an officer on *Orion*'s bridge remarked to a companion, 'What's that battleship over there? I thought ours were miles away.' At 1055, *Vittorio Veneto* joined the Italian cruisers and immediately opened fire on the shadowing Allied cruisers. Admiral Cunningham launched a series of three aerial attacks, the second of which damaged the *Vittorio Veneto*. The second attack achieved one torpedo hit on the cruiser *Pola*, which had nearly stopped to avoid running into *Fiume* and could not take any evasive action. This blow knocked out five boilers and the main steam line,

Perth during 1941/42. Note the accommodation ladder deployed on the starboard quarter and the sailing boat alongside.

Perth in the Mediterranean in mid-1941. The anti-rangefinding baffles on the funnels can just be made out. *(Naval Photograph Club)*

causing *Pola* to lose electric power and drift to a stop.

At 2015, *Orion*'s radar picked up a ship six miles to port, apparently dead in the water – the crippled *Pola*. The bulk of the Allied forces detected the Italian squadron on radar shortly after 2200 and were able to close without being detected. The battleships were able to close to 3800 yards, at which point they opened fire. After just three minutes, *Fiume* and *Zara* had been destroyed. Two Italian destroyers were also sunk in the first five minutes. *Pola*'s crew was taken off and she was sunk by torpedoes from the destroyers *Jervis* and *Nubian* shortly after 0400.

PERTH AND THE BATTLE OF SUNDA STRAIT

The Japanese invasion of the Dutch East Indies progressed swiftly and, at the end of February 1942, the Japanese were preparing to strike at Java. During a series of fierce night encounters in the Java Sea, the Allies lost the majority of their ships, which were attempting to attack the invasion force, leaving just *Perth* and the American heavy cruiser *Houston*.

Perth and *Houston* retired to Tanjung Priok where, on 28 February they received orders to sail through the Sunda Strait to Tjilatjap. They encountered the main Japanese invasion fleet and, during a night engagement, were both sunk.

LOSS OF *SYDNEY*

Returning from her convoy duties to Java, *Sydney* was proceeding south along the northwest coast of Western Australia when she sighted what appeared to be a merchant vessel at about 1600 on 19 November 1941, some 130 miles west of Shark Bay.

The ship was in fact the German raider *Kormoran*. *Sydney* challenged the vessel continuously using her searchlight while at

The German raider *Kormoran* meets a U-boat at sea.

the same time closing the range between the two ships. Merchant vessels were known to be less efficient at visual signalling and the Germans exploited this knowledge through their actions on their flag deck and by their slow response to *Sydney*'s visual challenges. At 1700, to further the deception, *Kormoran* broadcast a 'suspicious ship' message, feigning a cry for help in the name of *Straat Malakka*.

Sydney's efforts to establish the true identity of the vessel resulted in her closing the range to a point where she no longer had the advantage of her superior armament. At approximately 1715 *Sydney* had drawn almost abeam of *Kormoran* to starboard, less than a mile distant. Both ships were steering west southwest at about 15 knots. Still wary, the Australian cruiser kept her main armament trained on the mysterious ship and her amphibious aircraft was on the catapult with its engine running. She then signalled, both by flags and flashing light; 'Where bound?' *Kormoran* replied 'Batavia'. The crucial moment then came when *Sydney* hoisted a two-flag signal consisting of the letters 'IK' which the raider could not interpret. They were in fact the two centre letters of the *Straat Malakka*'s four-letter secret identification signal (IIKP). With no reply forthcoming *Sydney* signalled in plain language 'Show your secret sign'.

Right and below: Two views of *Sydney* in Sydney Harbour in 1941, nine months before she was lost.

Finally, when concealment of his vessel's true identity was no longer possible, and with the advantage of surprise, the German captain Theodor Detmers ordered the Dutch colours to be struck, hoisted the German naval ensign and at approximately 1730 opened fire with all armament at a range 'somewhat more than a mile'.

It is likely that the raider's first salvo destroyed *Sydney*'s bridge, with the result that her primary control was immediately put out of action. *Sydney*'s own guns opened fire almost simultaneously with a full salvo that passed over *Kormoran* without inflicting damage. *Kormoran* again scored hits on *Sydney* with two salvos again hitting her bridge and midships section. According to the Germans all of *Kormoran*'s armament was brought to bear on *Sydney*, concentrating on her bridge, torpedo tubes and anti-aircraft batteries.

For a few seconds after her initial salvo *Sydney* did not reply. It appears that her forward 'A' and 'B' turrets were put out of action leaving only her after turrets 'X' and 'Y' to respond. It was reported by the Germans that *Sydney*'s 'X' turret opened fast and accurate fire, hitting *Kormoran* in the funnel and engine room. 'Y' turret is said to have fired only two or three salvos,

all of which went over. At about this time one of the raider's two torpedoes struck *Sydney* under 'A' and 'B' turrets. The other passed close ahead of the stricken ship, which was subjected to enfilading fire.

With her bow low in the water, *Sydney* then turned sharply towards *Kormoran* as though attempting to ram. As she did so, the top of 'B' turret was blown off and flew overboard, the cruiser then passed under *Kormoran*'s stern, heading to the southward and losing way. *Kormoran*, maintaining her course and speed, was now on fire in the engine room where hits by *Sydney*'s 'X' turret had caused severe damage. Smoke from the fire hid *Sydney* from *Kormoran*'s bridge but the raider continued to engage with her after guns as the range opened to approximately 4400 yards.

At about 1745 *Sydney* was seen to fire a torpedo when Detmers was turning his ship to port to bring his broadside to bear, but as he did so *Kormoran*'s engines began to fail. The torpedo track was sighted and it was subsequently avoided. Simultaneously the raider's engines broke down completely.

Sydney, crippled and on fire from the bridge to the after funnel, steamed slowly to the south returning only sporadic fire from her secondary armament. Although by now the range had opened to 6600 yards *Sydney* continued to receive steady hits from *Kormoran*'s port broadside. At 1800, at a range of 7700 yards, *Kormoran* then fired one torpedo that missed *Sydney*'s stern. Although this fierce action had lasted only half an hour both ships had been dealt mortal blows.

Kormoran fired her last shot at 1825 at a range of about 11,000 yards. The Germans claim to have fired approximately 450 rounds from her main armament and hundreds from her anti-aircraft batteries. With the gathering gloom the form of *Sydney* disappeared from view and was last seen by the Germans about ten miles off, heading approximately south southeast. Thereafter, until about 2200, all that was seen was a distant glare then occasional flickerings until midnight at which time all trace of *Sydney* disappeared.

The wrecks of *Sydney* and *Kormoran*, and the associated debris fields, are located 22 kilometres apart, 290 kilometres west southwest of Carnarvon, off the

The location of the wrecks of *Sydney* and *Kormoran*.

View of *Hobart* at Espiritu Santo, New Hebrides. Photographed from the port side, showing the ship's badly distorted stern, after 6in gun turrets, anti-splinter mats on the after superstructure and surface search radar Type 271 at left. (*US Naval History and Heritage Command, NH 80532*)

Penelope, riddled by shrapnel after heavy bombing while at Malta in March 1942, and further bombing on her way to Gibraltar for repairs.

coast of Western Australia in 2500 metres of water.

HOBART AND ASSAULT LANDINGS IN THE SOLOMONS

On 20 July 1943, *Hobart* was torpedoed by the Japanese submarine *Ro-106* while en route to Espiritu Santo, Vanuatu, as part of Task Force 74. The torpedo struck aft on the port side causing considerable damage in the vicinity of the wardroom. Thirteen officers and sailors were killed and another seven injured. She made it to Espiritu Santo under her own power the following day where she underwent temporary repairs and was escorted to Sydney by *Warramunga* and *Arunta*. She arrived on 26 August for extensive repairs which kept her out of service until December 1944. *Hobart* was finally broken up in 1962.

LOSS OF *PENELOPE*

Penelope was holed both forward and aft by near-misses during air attacks on Malta on 26 March 1942. While in the island, she was docked and repaired at the Malta Dry Docks. Day after day she was attacked by German aircraft and the crew worked to fix a myriad of shrapnel holes, so many that she was nicknamed 'Pepperpot'. When these had been plugged with long pieces of wood, she was re-named 'Porcupine'.

In February 1944, *Penelope*, with the ships of Force 'X', carried out five bombardments in support of military operations at Anzio beachhead. On the 17th, during passage to Naples to replenish ammunition, she was hit by an acoustic torpedo (T5) fired from *U-410*, 35 miles west of Naples off Cape Circe. *Penelope* sank 10 minutes after a further torpedo attack by *U-410* which caused a major explosion; 415 of the ships' company were lost with 250 survivors being rescued by landing craft.

LOSS OF *GALATEA*

On 13 December 1941, following the bombardment of Derna, *Galatea*, together with the cruisers *Euryalus* and *Naiad*, joined Force 'K' from Malta, to intercept an enemy supply convoy on passage from Taranto to North Africa. The next day, the operation was cancelled as the convoy had been recalled. *Galatea* rejoined Force 'B' for the return voyage to Alexandria, but on the 15th she was hit by a salvo of torpedoes fired by *U-557* whilst entering the swept channel 30 miles NW of Alexandria. *Galatea* sank in three minutes. There were 150 survivors rescued by the destroyers *Griffin* and *Hotspur*.

Penelope in 1944, shortly before being sunk. She wore the same camouflage scheme at the time of her sinking.

Model Products

NAVIS-NEPTUN

1:1250 scale

This German company produces the largest range of 1:1250 scale metal models, including ships from many countries, and of many eras. The range is so large that not all models can be in production at any one time, frequently resulting in long waiting times when a modeller requires a specific model.

Currently, the range includes: 1144 *Penelope*; 1145 *Perth*; 1146 *Ajax*; 1146a *Achilles*; 1146aS *Achilles* white-buff. They are normally painted grey overall, with highlights such as black funnel tops and brown tops to boats. 1146aS was a limited run. The details are fine, and the model details are generally accurate.

MOUNTFORD MODELS

1:1250 scale

Based in Britain, Mountford marketed their models either as kits to be built by individual modellers, or as assembled and painted models. Most of their kits were manufactured in metal, but some of their later ones had resin hulls. They were not very accurate or finely detailed, masts and gun barrels being noticeably oversize. Although advertised as being at 1:1250 scale, the hull of *Ajax* is slightly longer than the Eaglewall model at 1:1200 scale. The size of the location holes for the missing quadruple 0.5in. gun mounts gives a clear indication of the crude moulding.

EAGLEWALL PLASTICS LTD

1:1200 scale

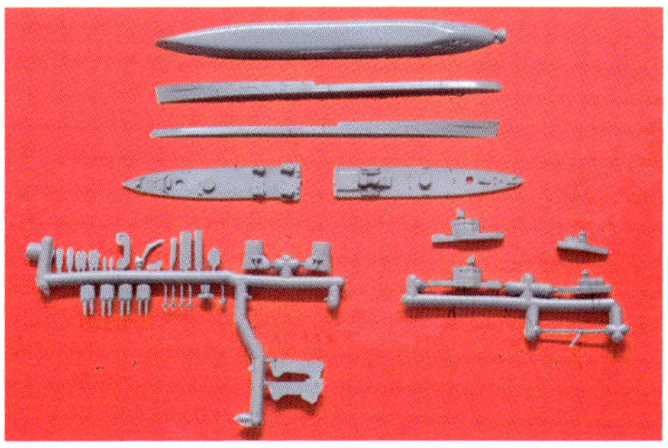

The Dorking-based company, Eaglewall Plastics Ltd, produced the Eagle range of plastic kits between 1958 and 1962, having moved to Brighton in 1960. They were well respected for their detail and accuracy, although moulding techniques of the time had a great number of limitations. This probably shows most clearly in the thickness of the masts.

HMS *Achilles* was part of the 'Battle of the River Plate' series, which included the sister-ship *Ajax* (identical mouldings), the heavy cruiser *Exeter*, and the German *Admiral Graf Spee*. Another sister-ship, *Orion*, was produced as part of the 'Battle of Cape Matapan' series. The instructions include a brief description of the battle, an assembly diagram and a general arr-

angement drawing with ten sectional views.

The above-water section of the hull is moulded in two parts, with a single piece below water. The deck is provided in two parts also, the forward section having the four 4in guns moulded integrally. At 140mm, the hull is spot-on for length. The other components are provided on two very thick sprues. The major parts, superstructure and funnel, are each provided in two halves. The 6in turrets are provided complete with barrels. There is a small amount of flash, which can be difficult to remove on very small components.

SKYTREX

1:700 scale

Another British company, Skytrex produce a number of metal warship models – 1:350 scale World War II Royal Navy warships and 1:700 scale modern 'fast attack craft' from a variety of different navies. Their 1:700 scale World War II Royal Navy warships are no longer listed.

The model of *Ajax* (MD4) is finely cast, with the exception of the masts, which are oversize and devoid of any yards. The model is painted grey overall, with a black funnel top and anchor chains. The gun barrels of the quadruple 0.5in mounts are also painted black, and the carley floats ochre. The wooden areas of the deck are indicated with oversize plank scribing. No aircraft is included.

NNT MODELL + BUCH

1:700 scale

This German model (70008) represents *Sydney* in her early career with four single 4in guns, and comprises a waterline resin hull, four packets of resin components, a small sheet of etched metal, and a small sheet of decals. The hull is cleanly moulded with just a small amount of curvature that can be easily removed. Its length is 237mm overall, about 7mm undersize. It includes the lower levels of superstructure.

There are three 'sprues', each containing three boats, two of which are identical. Only six of these boats are used, another two being provided on separate sprues, alongside the quad torpedo tubes. The torpedo tubes are bare and could be replaced with 'after-market' parts. The bridge moulding includes windows for the open bridge. These need to be painted on both sides or removed and replaced by acetate sheet for a realistic appearance. A canopy is provided but not illustrated in the instructions. The rangefinders on the open bridge are missing. The superstructure platforms are provided on a resin wafer, with the boat support frames on another, smaller one.

The two funnel mouldings are identical but their bases, which are included on the superstructure mouldings, result in their heights being different when complete. The funnels are moulded solid and should be drilled out and funnel grilles added to increase realism. The four 6in turrets are supplied with a total of ten barrels, and six 4in barrels are supplied for the four mounts. Four small gun mouldings are supplied with their barrels elevated to 45° and the assembly drawing shows them to be fitted on the platform at the base of the mainmast. It is assumed these are meant to represent the 3pdr saluting guns and are best omitted. The aircraft is supplied in three parts – a forward section and lower wing, a tail section and an upper wing. Carley floats and searchlights are included, as are chocks for the boats.

The main items on the etched metal sheet are the crane and the aircraft catapult. There are also crossed supports for the platforms and boats, davits, ladders and anchors with anchor chains, but no railings. The sheet also includes the quad

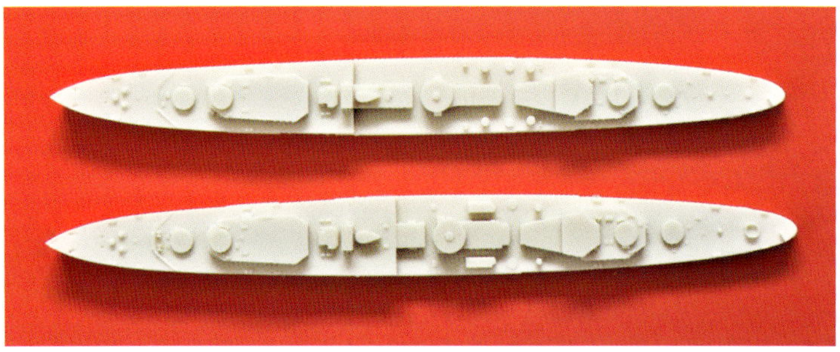

0.5in machine guns, which should be replaced with 'after-market' mouldings. The decals include a white ensign, ship names and roundels for the aircraft.

Instructions are brief on three A4 and one A5 sheet, all single-sided. They include basic technical information in German and English, and an assembly diagram. The A5 sheet includes a chart of the famous engagement with the German raider *Kormoran*. Assembly of items such as the crane are not clear, the crane comprising three items from the etched metal sheet and one resin part. The assembly diagram includes drawings of the masts, which have to be made from brass rod (not supplied), giving heights but no diameters.

There are no painting instructions but *Profile Morskie 65* does include a camouflage drawing of *Sydney* as at June 1941.

Another model in this series (70031) can be assembled in a number of different configurations, representing HMAS *Perth* at different times in her career. The waterline hull is similar to that supplied for *Sydney*, but there are differences, the most noticeable being the position of the forecastle break, which is further aft. Other differences are reflected in the different mouldings supplied, *eg* there are no open bridge windows moulded onto the bridge. The etched metal sheet is larger, but guardrails are not included. The decal sheet is the same, but there is also a supplementary one containing smaller ensigns.

The assembly diagram shows *Perth* as in 1942, although the text refers to a number of different configurations. Alternative parts are supplied in the kit, and profile drawings of *Perth* as in 1939 and 1941 are included, but the modeller must carry out more research to identify precise details. More painting details are included, but again more research is required; *Profile Morskie 66* does include a camouflage drawing of *Perth* as in February 1942. Some of the details could be replaced by 'after-market' items to enhance the appearance.

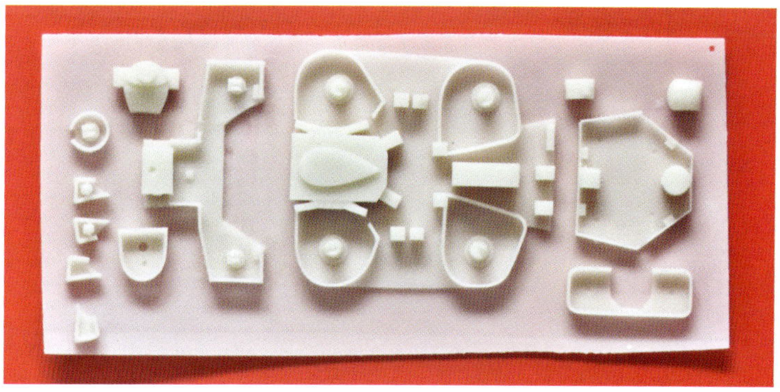

HP MODELS

1:700 scale

This German company offers kits of three of the *Leander* class. The kit WWII-WL-GB-095 represents *Ajax* as in 1942, having had her hull sides extended to reduce wetness, the four single 4in guns replaced by twins, the catapult removed, the smaller AA weapons increased, and the pole masts replaced by tripods.

The kit comprises a cleanly cast, waterline resin hull, with no signs of warping, three resin wafers containing the superstructure parts, the gun turrets, the boats, and other small details, plus two separate wafers, one containing the bridge and the other, the funnel. There is no flash on the last two, and only very thin flash on the other three. With a length of 240mm, the hull is just 1.5mm short. There is no etched brass sheet, items such as the crane being moulded in resin with surface detail representing the lattice metal structure, but there is a small sheet containing flags, white ensigns and admirals' flags.

The modeller must supply the masts, but the instructions do include both length and diameter. The instructions also include a diagram showing the parts in the kit, an assembly diagram and a general arrangement drawing. There are no painting instructions, but she did wear a very

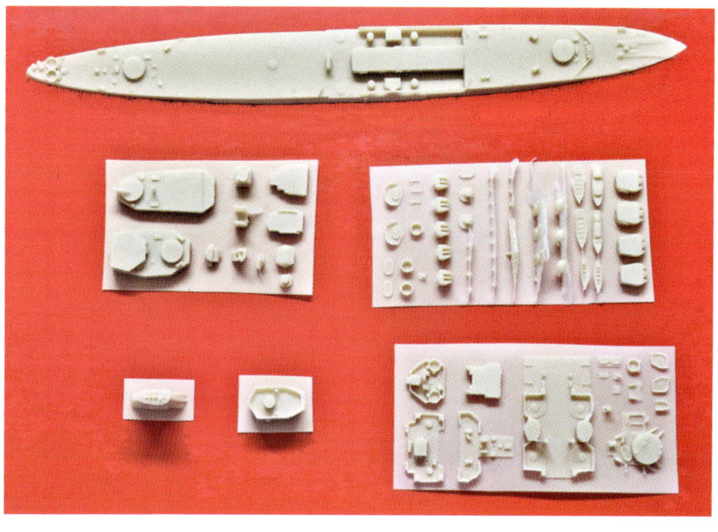

noticeable camouflage scheme at the time – see *Profile Morskie 1*.

The addition of some etched brass for guardrails and to replace the various lattice structures, will make a significant improvement.

The same comments apply to the kit of *Orion*, which represents the cruiser as in 1943 after her catapult had been removed, but in this case a colour drawing, of a much simpler scheme, is included, but the colours are not identified.

The model of *Neptune* represents the vessel as in 1936. It includes both Hawker Osprey and Fairey Seafox aircraft, one with wings folded. No colour details are provided, but mast dimensions are given.

B-RESINA

1:700 scale

This Czech kit (BR707) is no longer in production and represents *Ajax* after having had her hull sides extended to reduce wetness, and the four single 4in guns replaced by twins. She retains her catapult, the smaller AA weapons remains at three quad 0.5in mountings, and the pole masts have been replaced by tripods.

The kit comprises a waterline resin hull, with three other large resin mouldings – the funnel and two superstructure blocks. The other resin components supplied include the boats and davits, the aircraft, the masts, the gun turrets with barrels and the crane is moulded on a resin wafer with surface detail representing the lattice metal structure. There is no photo-etch.

The instructions are supplied on a single sheet and include diagrams showing the parts in the kit, and an assembly

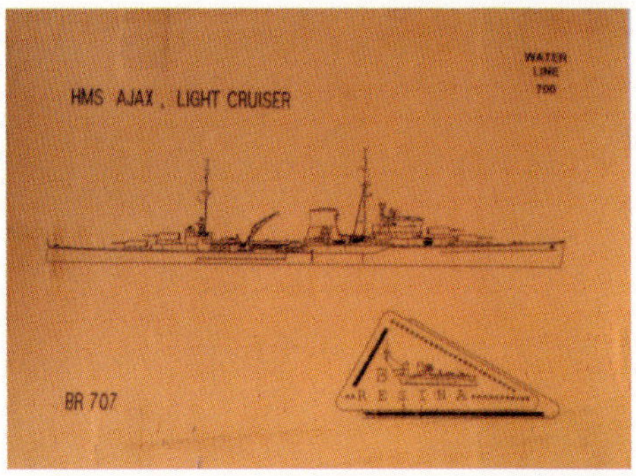

diagram/general arrangement drawing. The colour scheme given is light grey overall with wooden decks and a dark grey forecastle.

The addition of some etched brass for guardrails, and to replace the various lattice structures, will make a significant improvement.

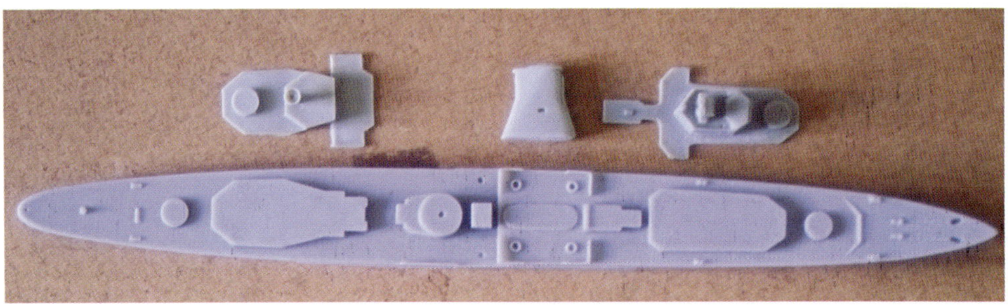

FLYHAWK

1:700 scale

Chinese Flyhawk kits are available in two forms – standard and deluxe. The plastic components in both are the same, but the deluxe version includes small sheets of etched brass, brass gun barrels and 3D printed parts. The additional parts are also available separately for those wishing to upgrade the standard version. The etched brass sheets include a range of details, including guardrails and lattice structures, such as cranes. The deluxe version of *Ajax* also includes tapered brass masts and lengths of brass rod. The deluxe version of *Aurora* (1945) also includes lengths of brass rod.

The kits are all similar in format,

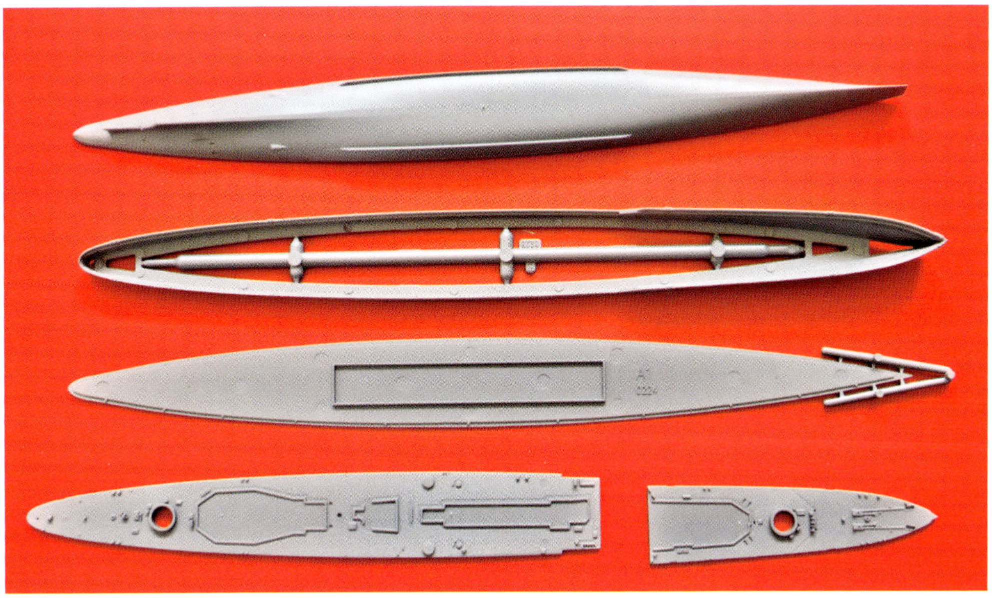

providing the options of a full-hull or waterline model, the above-water section of the hull is moulded in a single piece. The many components are all cleanly moulded and well detailed. Standard sprues are provided for many common items, such as close-range AA weapons, and so there are frequently spare parts available.

A sheet of decals is included, providing white ensigns and roundels for the aircraft. Also there is a 'lead weight' which fits on the waterline plate, to add stability to a waterline model if desired.

Inside the box is a reproduction of the box top artwork and extensive instructions. These are provided in the form of pictorial diagrams, on a long, double-sided sheet of paper. Colour details are provided, with paints nominated from the Mr Hobby, Tamiya and Colourcoats ranges.

FH1110 represents *Ajax* as in 1939, still with pole masts but after the twin 4in AA guns were installed. She is painted grey 507C overall, but a camouflage scheme is supplied for the Fairey Seafox aircraft.

Galatea (FH1158) is represented just

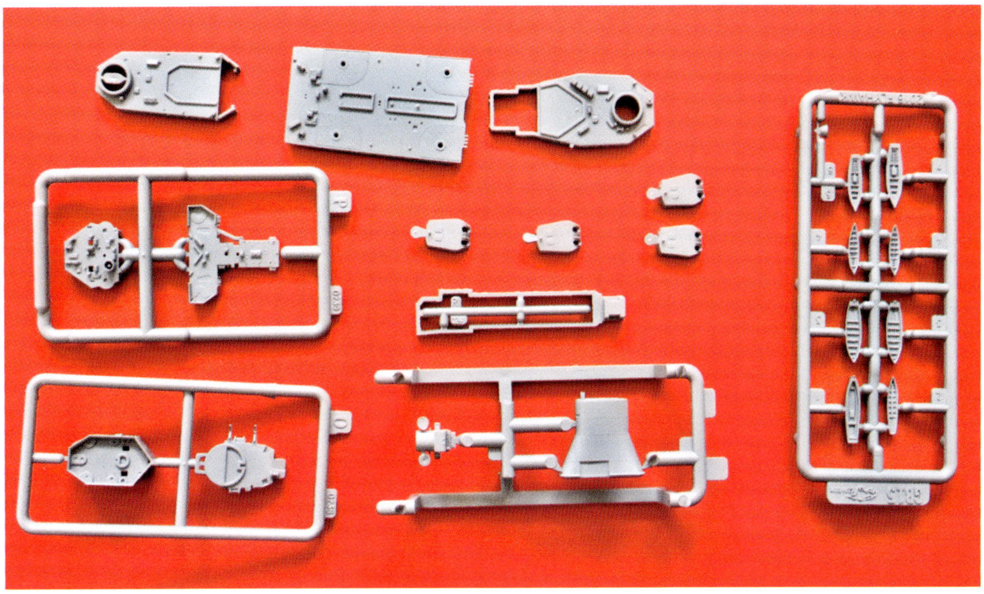

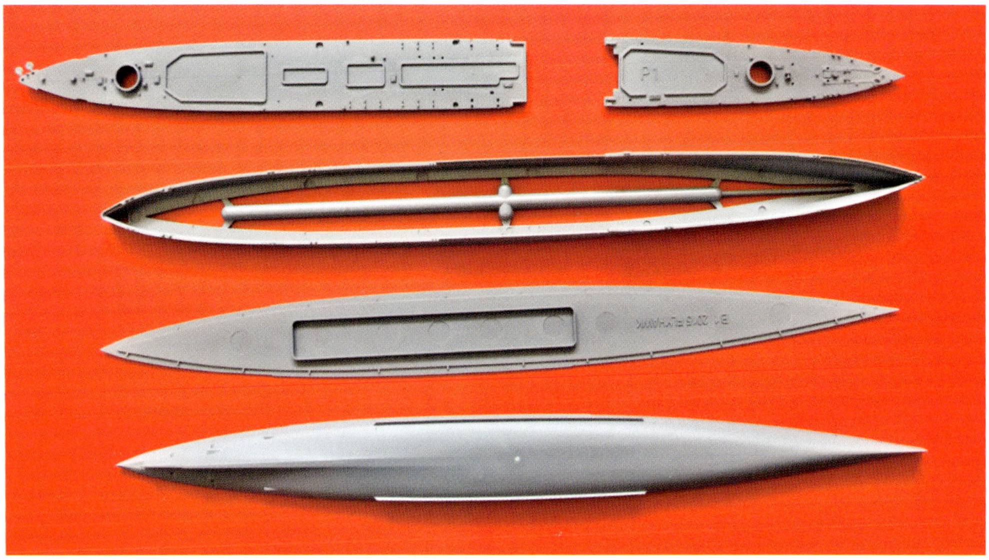

prior to WWII, wearing neutrality stripes on 'B' turret. She is also painted grey 507C overall, and again a camouflage scheme is supplied for the Fairey Seafox aircraft, which can be displayed with the wings either folded or deployed.

Penelope (FH1109) is portrayed in a striking camouflage scheme worn in 1940.

The option of either a Fairey Seafox or Supermarine Walrus aircraft is included.

Aurora is provided either as in 1941 or 1945 (FH1157 and FH1127). In 1941 she was painted in 'Mountbatten Pink', and in 1945 she was grey with a dark hull panel and tripod masts. No aircraft were carried at either time.

These will all make into fine models, but do have a high component count, requiring much patience, and more than a little skill to complete satisfactorily.

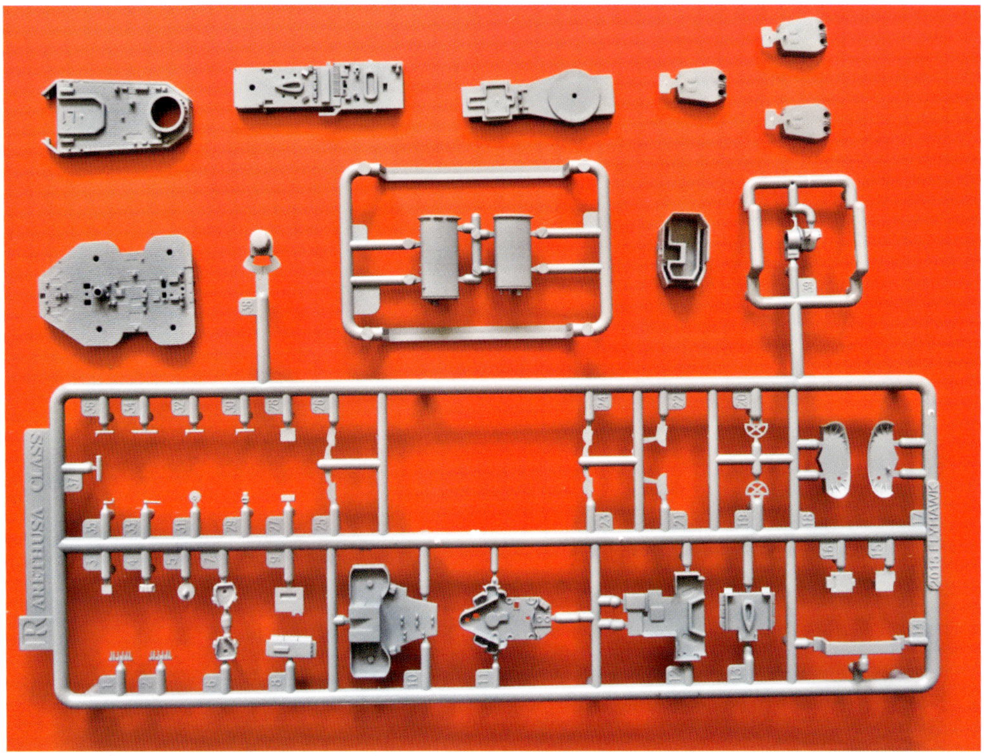

WHITE ENSIGN MODELS

1:700 scale

Prior to the change of ownership and subsequent relocation to the USA, WEM released a model of *Penelope* as in 1940. The kit included a waterline resin hull, with three plastic bags of smaller resin components, including the superstructure, funnels and armament. There were two lengths of different diameter brass rod for the masts and a small etched brass sheet, which included the aircraft catapult, the crane boom, yards, boat chocks and davits, but no guardrails. This sheet is currently available as PE707. The instructions included the dimensions for the masts, as well as full colour details, the paints coming from the Colourcoats range.

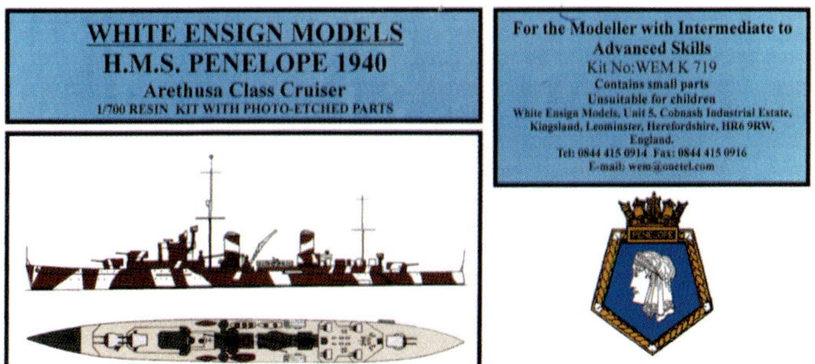

"Constantia et Fide"

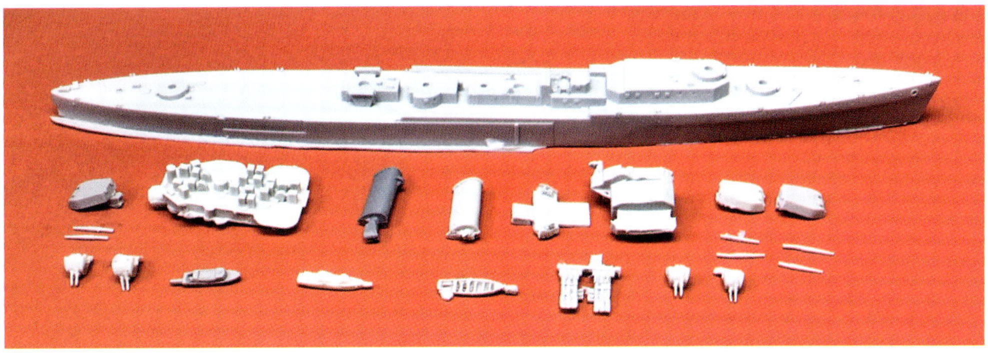

AIRFIX

1:600 scale

The kit of HMS *Ajax* was first released by this venerable British company in 1965, and has been re-released a number of times, the only significant changes being to the box and the box top artwork. It is a series 3 kit, rated at skill level 2.

In common with most other manufacturers of the period, the full-hull is provided in two parts, port and starboard, with a two-piece deck, which includes the bulkheads of the first superstructure level. The funnel and bridge are both moulded in two halves, and the turrets have separate gun barrels. A stand is included for display of a full-hull model. Assembly instructions are given in 13 diagrams, with colours for *Ajax* as at the Battle of the River Plate. This does highlight an error in the kit, which includes a tripod foremast, rather than a pole mast.

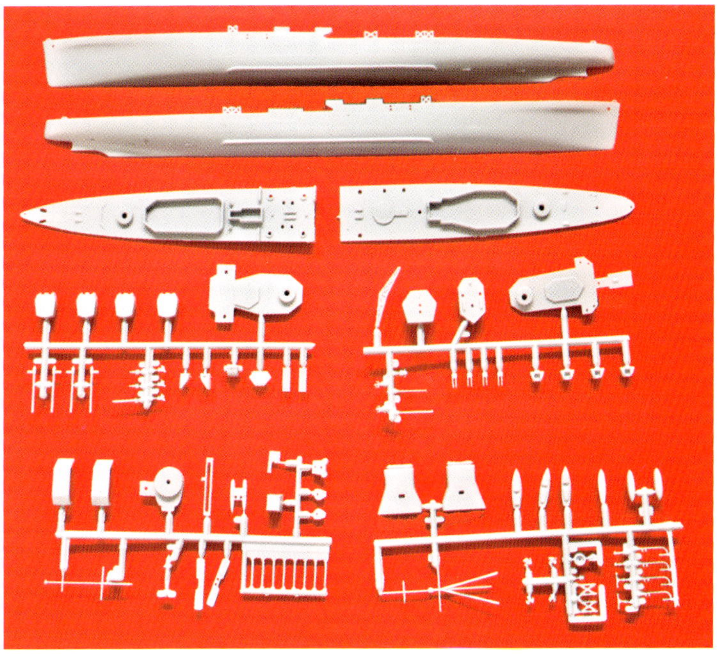

The components are cleanly moulded, with little flash, and the masts are quite fine, although the limitations in the moulding process of the time does limit the amount of detail included. The kit forms a good basis for creation of an accurate, detailed model.

WYDAWNICTWO JSC 1:400 scale

This Polish card model of *Penelope* is provided in an A4 book (57), together with a model of the frigate HMS *Spey*. As well as a Supermarine Walrus for use on board *Penelope*, a model of a Short Sunderland is also included.

There are two pages of technical and historical details of the two ships, firstly in Polish and secondly in English. There are also two pages of assembly instructions, also in both languages. On the front cover is an artist's impression of *Penelope*, and inside, a general arrangement drawing of the model, showing the location of components, and the size of masts. Six pages of coloured card contain the components for both vessels, the two aircraft being printed on the back cover.

Ajax/Achilles is also included in an A4 size book (404), but with illustrations of the card model on the front. Technical details of *Ajax*, and assembly instructions are given in both Polish and English. There are also four pages of assembly diagrams.

The model components are contained on six pages of coloured card, and details of the masts and gun barrels are given on the back cover. Two thinner half-pages contain the components for a Fairey Seafox (*Ajax*) and a Supermarine Walrus (*Achilles*).

IRON SHIPWRIGHTS 1:350 scale

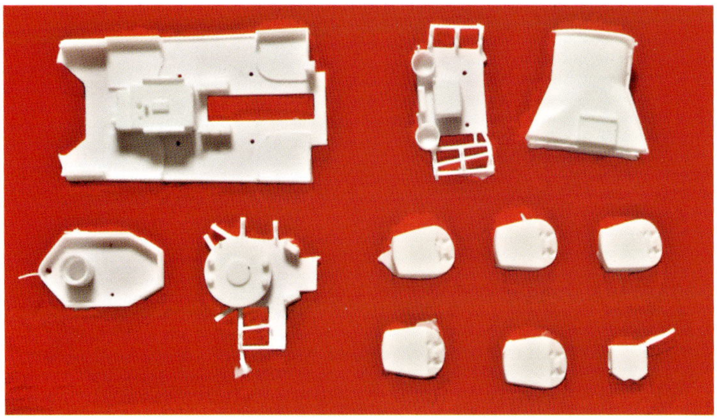

This American company produces a full-hull, resin moulding of *Ajax* (4-230), with the hull including the main parts of the superstructure, along with the bridge. The hull is cleanly moulded, with cleaning-up being required along the centreline, on the bottom of the hull. The bilge keels are poorly moulded and will require considerable reworking if the modeller wishes to display a full-hull model. The main parts of the superstructure and primary gun turrets are also cleanly moulded, requiring only a little cleaning-up, but the smaller details have a lot of flash to be removed before they can be used.

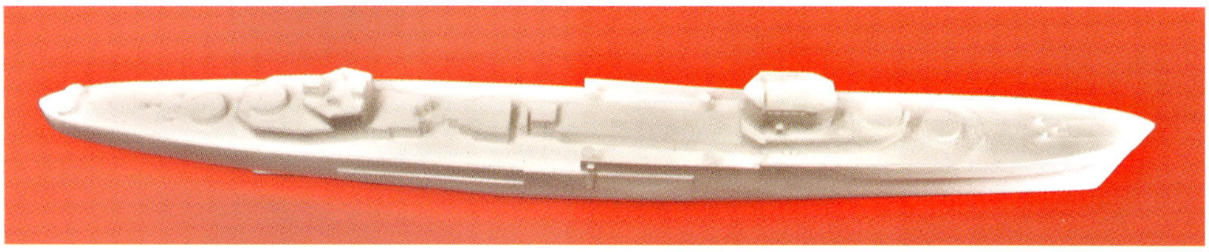

There is also an extensive etched brass sheet, and brass rod of various diameters for the masts, although resin masts are also included. Instructions are provided in a pictorial format, on nine pages. The model represents *Ajax* as in early 1941, while she still retained her catapult, a Supermarine Walrus aircraft being included in the kit. However, the hull moulding includes two drums for Oerlikon 20mm guns right aft, which suggests a 1942 fit, after the catapult was removed and replaced with a quad pom-pom. Other details also need to be checked for an accurate model. A general assembly drawing is provided on the last page of the instructions, but no colour details are included.

This kit provides a good basis for an accurate model, although replacement of some details by after-market parts will greatly enhance the result.

CHUAN YU

1:200 scale

This Chinese kit of HMS *Aurora* is one of a series of 1:200 scale models which are produced using 3D printing techniques, and so there is very little cleaning-up and the fit of parts is very good. Being one of the larger models in the series, *Aurora* is intended for radio control, and hence the kit includes four electric motors, four shafts and four propellers.

As well as the 3D printed components, there is a self-adhesive wooden deck, an extensive amount of etched brass, and some brass rod. Instructions are provided in pictorial format, but no colour details are included. A very light wooden stand is included for the model, but is really only suitable for a temporary support whilst building the model.

FLEETSCALE

1:96 scale

For those wishing to build a larger, working model, Fleetscale of the UK produce a GRP 'WW2 HMS *Orion* Hull (Modified *Leander*)', which features armour markings, propeller outlets, bilge keels and port hole indents. It can be obtained either with or without a flange on the edge (JH/96/1/MLCCWW2HNF, JH/96/1/ML CCWW2HF).

It is understood that the term 'Modified Leander' applies to the size of the hull reflecting the increased beam of the later cruisers.

ACCESSORIES
PHOTO-ETCH

Common items, such as guardwires and ladders, are widely available in all the scales commonly used by modellers from: Gold Medal Models, Tom's Modelworks and White Ensign Models in the USA, Atlantic Models and Starling Models in the UK, L'Arsenal in France, and Eduard in Germany.

WHITE ENSIGN MODELS 1:600 scale

The photo-etch sheet for *Ajax* (PE 617) was originally produced in the UK and released in 1999. It was designed to fit the Airfix kit for a late pre-war/early WWII fit, and is still available from the USA.

It contains the following components: crane jib, crane turntable, crane cab, foremast rigging, mainmast rigging, funnel cap grill, upper funnel siren platforms, catapult turntable, cutter cradles, catapult, aircraft launch trolley, accommodation ladders, catapult turntable surround, 0.5in quad machine guns, whaler davits, motor boat cradles, large deck hatches, bridge rangefinders, anchor cables, vertical & inclined ladders, sundry hatches, waffle pattern doors, anchors, Fairey Seafox parts, searchlight platform crossbraces, whaler cradles, whaler rudders & oars, whaler thwarts, cutter thwarts, HACS director forward bracing, ensign staff, jackstaff, engine room vent grills, cutter sponson support bracing, aft motor boat sponson supports, forward quad MG sponson supports, 3-bar guardrails, 2-bar guardrails.

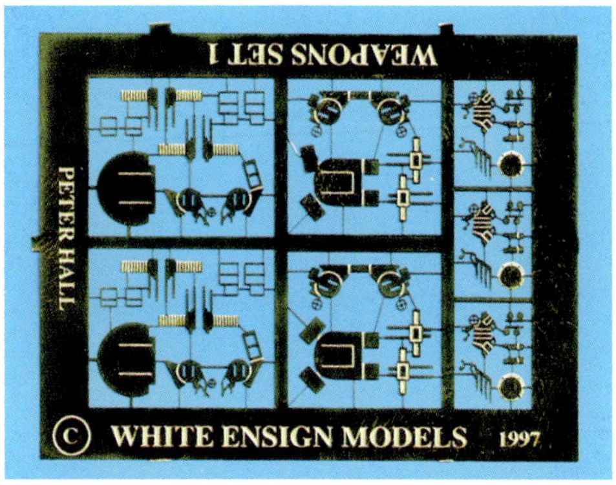

There is also a small photo-etch sheet 'WWII RN Light AA Weapons' (PE 613): 2 x 8-barrelled pom-poms, 2 x 4-barrelled pom-poms, 3 x 0.5in machine guns. It is described as containing multi-part designs in superb relief-etched 3-thou brass, for the experienced modeller only!! Some modellers dislike the 'flat' barrels which result from using photo-etch. It is also available at 1:700 scale as PE720.

TOM'S MODELWORKS 1:600 scale

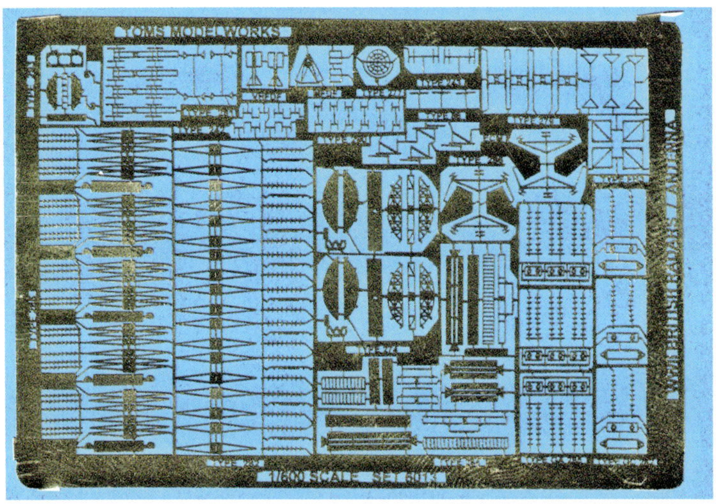

The small photo-etch sheet 'WWII British Radars/Antenna' (6013) contains a variety of radar and direction-finding antennas, including Types 279, 281 and 291 Air Warning Radars, Type 286 Surface Warning Radar, and Types 282, 283 and 285 Gunnery Control Radars, many of which were fitted to the *Leander* class and other light cruisers in their careers. The 'Headache' ECM and MF/DF and HF/DF antennas are also included. It is also available at 1:700 scale, item 738.

WOODEN DECKS

FLYHAWK

1:700 scale

Flyhawk produce a self-adhesive wooden deck for many of their kits: *Ajax* (FH710071), *Galatea* (FH7100610), *Penelope* (FH710023). These are very thin and have holes precisely cut to match the locations of the details moulded on the kit's deck. Note the differences between the sister ships *Galatea* and *Penelope*.

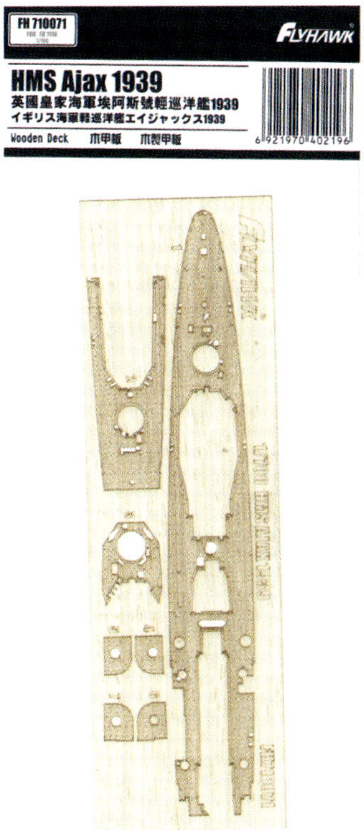

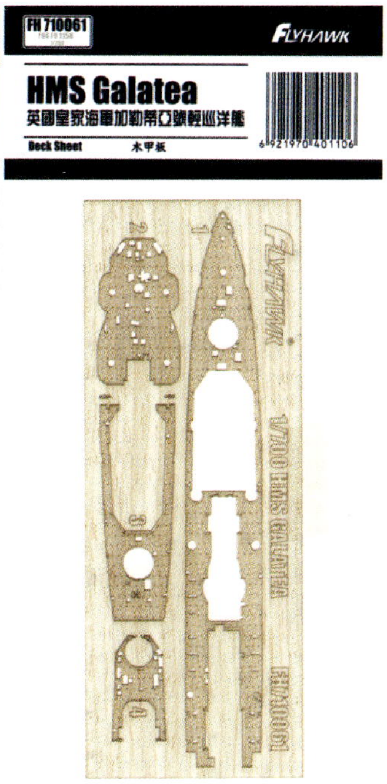

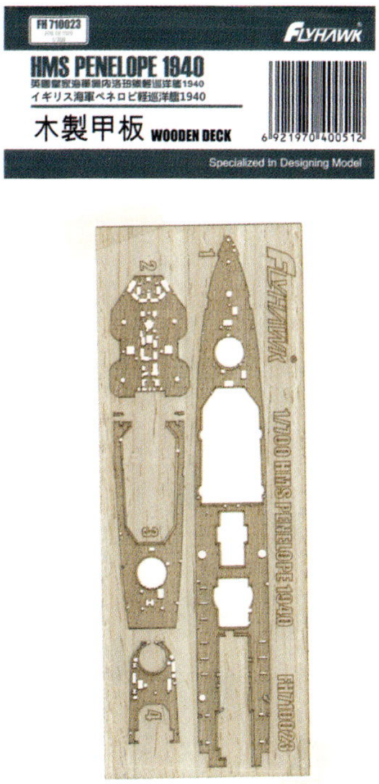

WOOD HUNTER

1:700 scale

Similar to the decks from Flyhawk, the American company Wood Hunter's *Aurora* (W70095) also includes a length of oversize anchor chain and a small, generic, brass sheet containing the supports for deck cable stowages.

FITTINGS

A large range of fittings is available at 1:700 scale, and, as 1:350 scale kits become more readily available and popular, so the range of accessories at that scale increases. The range mainly comprises boats, floats, small calibre guns, aircraft and depth charge throwers and rails. Earlier fittings were usually cast in resin, but recent developments in 3D printing have resulted in a great increase in available fittings. With the ability to easily scale the parts, this has also resulted in more scales becoming available for the fittings.

MICROMASTER

Various scales

MicroMaster began selling their 3D printed products via the Shapeways website, but now have their own production facilities in New Zealand. Many of their products are still available from Shapeways, but since starting their own production, MicroMaster have significantly increased their range, and the new items are only available direct. The Shapeways items are produced in a translucent material, but those from MicroMaster are in a grey material. Not only do they produce items in the popular scales for small scale models (*ie* 1:700, 1:600 & 1:350), but some

are also available at larger scales, such as 1:96 &1:72, used for working models.

Particular items of interest include a number of 1:600 scale parts for use with the Airfix model of *Ajax*. These include the bridge, the lower bridge superstructure, the aft superstructure, the funnel, the torpedo workshop, the directors and the turrets. Common items such as torpedo tubes, rangefinders, searchlights, boats and carley floats are also available. The superstructure parts moulded to the kit decks will need to be removed before the new parts are fitted.

A range of items at 1:350 scale that could be used to enhance the Iron Shipwrights kit are also available. These include a wide range of boats and carley floats. There is also a range of weapons available, including the twin 4in AA turrets, 20mm Oerlikon guns and quad 0.5in machine gun mounts. Of direct relevance to the *Leander* class cruisers are the twin 6in turrets, the HACS Mark III (either covered or uncovered or with Type 285 radar), the rangefinders, the QR Mark IV quadruple torpedo tubes, depth charge rails and the DCT Mark XXI director for the primary armament.

They are all very detailed and will enhance the original kit significantly.

STARLING MODELS

1:700 scale

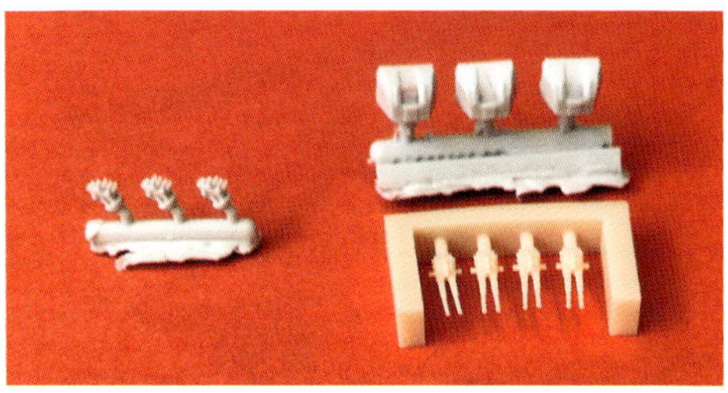

These items are produced by this British firm using 3D printing techniques, hence needing no cleaning-up. The range includes the quad 0.5in machine gun mounts (STA28) and the twin 4in AA mounts (STA31). The 0.5in mounts are a single piece whereas the twin 4in mount has a separate twin barrel assembly.

OZMODS

1:600 scale

OzMods of Australia market a packet of six resin 6in twin gun turrets to replace those in the Airfix kit of *Ajax*. These are cleanly moulded with additional detail, but with no gun barrels.

WHITE ENSIGN MODELS

1:700 and 1:600 scales

Before being taken over and moving to the USA, WEM (UK) produced a range of resin fittings at both 1:700 and 1:600 scales. As well as a variety of boats and gun mountings, at both scales, they also produced a Fairey IIIF aircraft at 1:600 scale (PRO607) and a 6/7-ton seaplane crane at 1:700 scale (PRO7044). Both of these included resin parts and a small sheet of photo-etch.

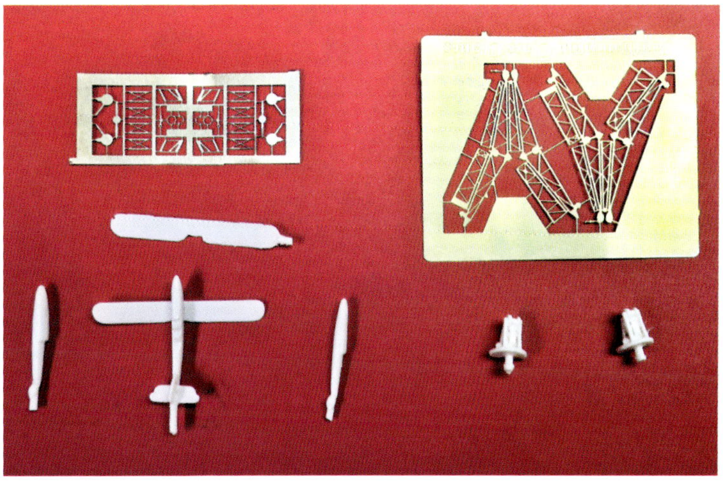

NIKO MODELS

1:700 scale

The Polish NIKO Models produce a range of resin fittings including the Vickers quad 0.5in MGs (ZW 7007B), the quad 2pdr pom-pom (ZW 7013B) and the twin 4in gun (ZW 7019B). The 0.5in guns are a single piece moulding, but the quad pom-pom comprises a base, gun barrel assembly and photo-etch railings. The twin 4in mounting comprises three resin parts – base, shield and twin barrels. All the resin parts contain flash and need some cleaning-up.

BLACK CAT MODELS

1:350 scale

Black Cat Models, of France, produce a range of 3D printed accessories that could be used to enhance the Iron Shipwrights kit. Unlike MicroMaster, armament is limited to small calibres, and includes the twin 4in mountings and 2pdr pom-poms.

A wide range of highly detailed boats and carley floats is also available, as are various ammunition and deck lockers.

TRUMPETER

1:350 scale

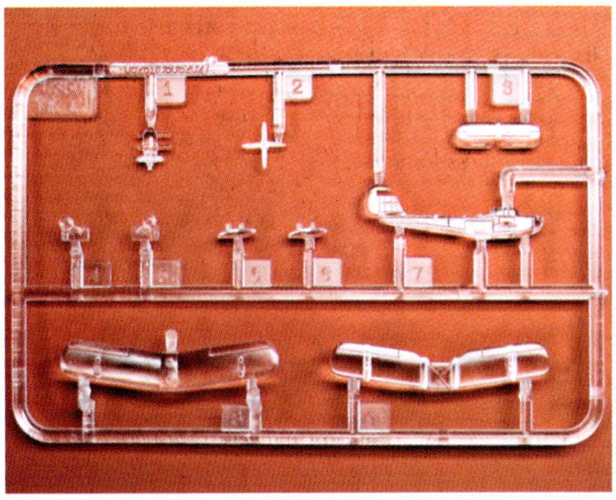

This well-known Chinese company produces a range of aircraft, including the Supermarine Walrus (06251). These are moulded in clear plastic so that the cockpit remains clear after painting. With the Walrus, the vertical sections between the wings are moulded solid and so need only struts painted on them, or, preferably, they should be replaced with photo-etch. Decals are included for the roundels on the wings and body, as are tail stripes but no painting details are given as these will, of course, depend on the particular aircraft being modelled.

Modelmakers' Showcase

SCRATCH-BUILT ***NEPTUNE*** 1:192 scale

Commission by ZAKOSKE

Andrew Parker's father, John Pechell Parker, served on *Neptune*, joining the ship during 1937 as a Paymaster Lieutenant, and not leaving the ship until July 1941. In the early 1980s, Andrew thought it might be nice to have a model made for his father's 70th birthday, his father's favourite ship being *Neptune*.

He contacted a firm of modelmakers, Zakoske, based in Hong Kong, all the workers employed there being disabled people. The model took nearly three years to complete. During this time, Andrew's father visited Zakoske on several occasions and discussed various details of *Neptune* and how these differed from the Admiralty plans.

This model depicts *Neptune* in her pre-war or early wartime days, painted overall AP 507C Light Admiralty Grey. She still carries the type EIIIH seaplane catapult with which she was originally fitted. Mounted on the catapult is a Fairey Seafox, the type which replaced the Hawker Osprey in August 1937. *Neptune* actually carried out the first sea trials of the Seafox at Gibraltar and shipped a pair of the aircraft from 716 Flight after her refit of March–September 1937. The catapult was removed in July 1941 and the space utilised for an additional anti-aircraft gun mounting. Note the locations of the four paravanes stored beside and behind 'B' turret. Just in front of the aft turrets is an elevated Vickers L62 quadruple anti-aircraft gun surrounded by railings.

NNT MODELL ***SYDNEY*** 1:700 scale

By DAVE EYLES

Dave made a few enhancements to this kit, including replacing the bridge windows with acetate sheet, adding rangefinders from FineMolds on the open bridge, and replacing the torpedo tubes with more detailed ones from NIKO. Funnel grilles came from a GMM photo-etch sheet, as did the guardwires. The primary gun turrets were replaced by 3D items from MicroMaster, and the quad 0.5in gun mountings by Flyhawk plastic parts. The boats came from L'Arsenal.

Profile Morskie 65 was used for colour details, and for the location of the guard-wires and smaller parts, such as the Carley floats.

NNT MODELL *SYDNEY* 1:700 scale

By DAVID GRIFFITH

This model is one of the case-studies in David Griffith's bestselling *Ship Models from Kits* (Seaforth Publishing) where building, enhancing, and painting the kit is described in detail.

HMAS SYDNEY
CRETE 1940

AIRFIX *AJAX* 1:600 scale

By FELIX BUSTELO

The model is about 20 years old now and showing some signs of age and warping of some of the WEM photo-etch, which is quite thin.

The venerable Airfix kit was completed using the old WEM dedicated photo-etch set and their resin Pro 600 replacements for the quad pom-pom and twin 4in secondary guns. Felix made numerous modifications to the model and added some scratch-built details. The model was painted in a dazzle scheme worn in 1941 when she was based in Alexandra, according to the first volume of Alan Raven's Camouflage series (see Bibliography).

SCRATCH-BUILT *AJAX* 1:96 scale

By GRAHAM BEESON

Graham has built four models of *Leander* class cruisers:

- *Neptune* at the time of her tragic loss.
- *Achilles* at the Battle of the River Plate.
- *Ajax* at the Battle of the River Plate.
- *Leander* in Philomel Dry Dock, Naval Base, Devonport, Auckland, NZ.

This model of *Ajax* was on display at the Royal New Zealand Navy Anniversary in October 2003, and all his models are now on display at the National Museum of the RNZN at Torpedo Bay in Auckland.

As the model depicts *Ajax* early in her career, there are no tripod masts, and amidships can be seen a Fairey Seafox on the catapult. Forward of the mainmast can been seen a second Seafox in the stowed position with its wings folded. Other points of interest are the single anchor on the port side, and on the main deck are two twin Vickers 4in anti-aircraft guns. The front face of *Ajax*'s bridge extends by 600mm (2ft), ¼ of an inch at 1:96 scale; the others had flush-front faced bridges.

AIRFIX *AJAX* 1:600 scale

By NIGEL DENCHFIELD

This model represents *Ajax* as at the Battle of The River Plate in 1939. Using the venerable Airfix kit as a basis resulted in a great deal of modifications, as well as generally cleaning-up the mouldings. Lattice structures were scratch-built for the platforms and crane jib. This conversion was carried out before the availability of 3D printed parts, and some of the later kits from Airfix were used to supply improved parts, the twin 4in guns coming from *Warspite*, for example. The Seafox aircraft required considerable attention to produce an acceptable representation.

SCRATCH-BUILT ***NEPTUNE*** 1:96 scale By GRAHAM BEESON

This model is almost six feet long and weighs about twelve pounds. Graham constructed the model based on a fibreglass hull with decks made of scale wood planking. He modelled the superstructure in wood first and then covered it with metal plate to accurately replicate the look of the original ship. The detailed fittings which complete the model are made from a variety of materials including metal as suited to their construction.

Because of the large scale of this model, the opportunity was taken to incorporate crew figures, which gives a great impression of the true size of the original ship. The 150 visible crewmen represent the 150 New Zealanders who died when the ship was lost, and a contingent of Royal Marines are on parade on the quarterdeck.

The model is now on display at the National Museum of the RNZN at Torpedo Bay in Auckland.

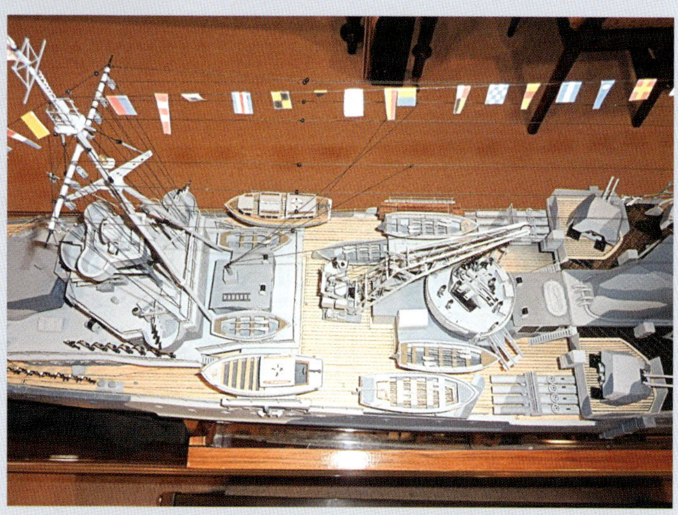

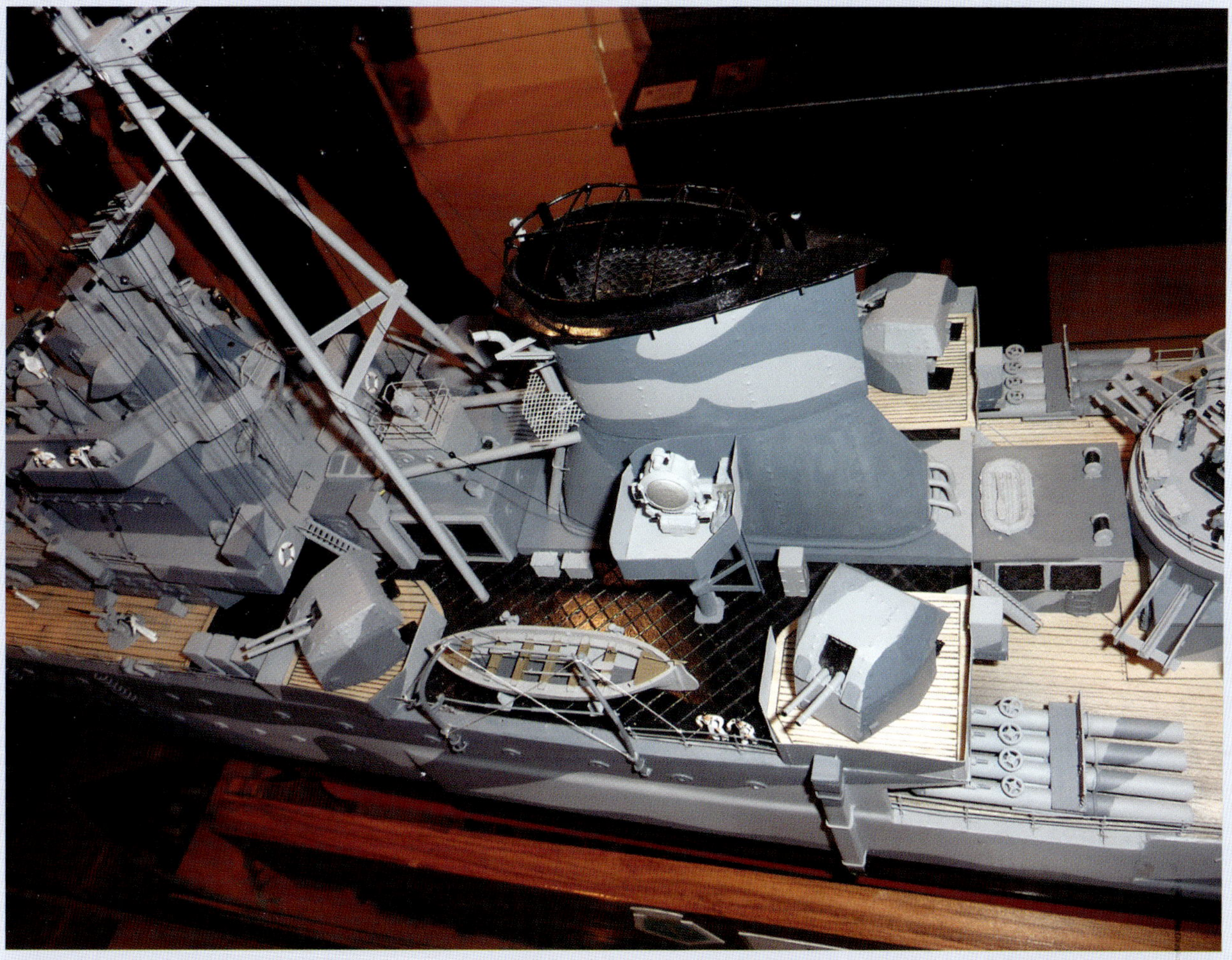

H. M. S. NEPTUNE

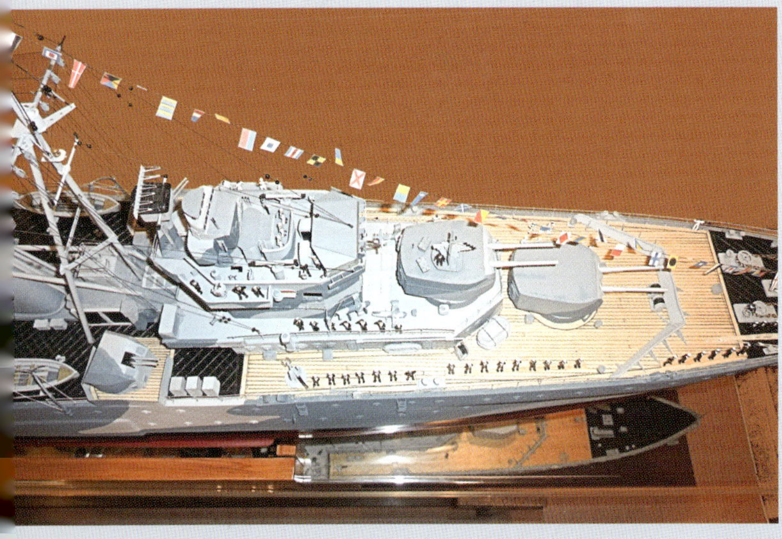

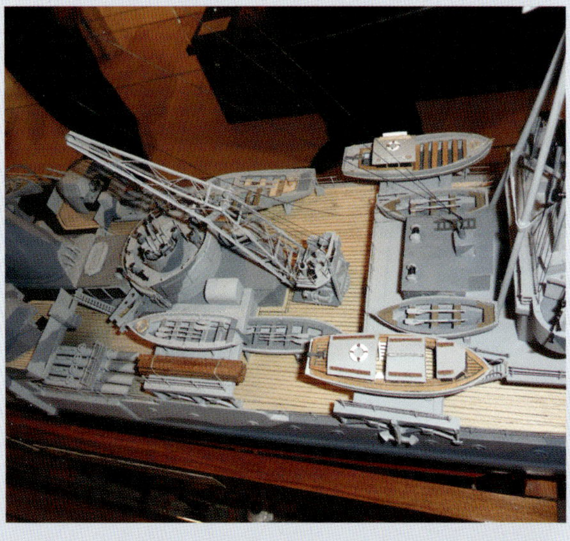

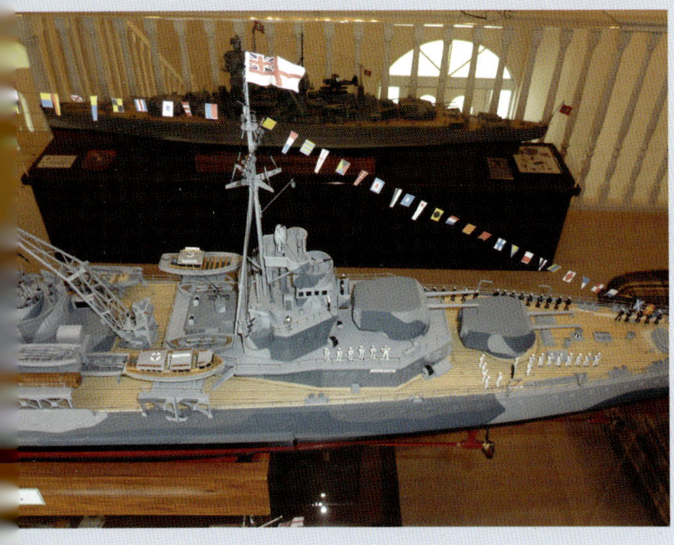

FLYHAWK *AJAX* 1:700 scale

By PETER FULGONEY

This model uses the deluxe version of the Flyhawk kit, including extra photo-etch and a wooden deck. The fitting is the 1941 Mediterranean black and light grey camouflage scheme, which is not represented in the kit. The Profile Morskie book (see Bibliography) gives the version Peter wanted to build, together with additional details and information to complete the model.

The kit is an exceptional product but will need an experienced modeller as the parts are numerous, very small and doubling up with the photo-etch provided. The camouflage work was started by using Xtradecal black lines to generate the splinter effect.

In conclusion, this kit is certainly worth the money but will need a steady hand and some experience for best results.

FLYHAWK ***AURORA*** 1:700 scale

By PETER FULGONEY

This is Peter's first build of a Flyhawk kit. He says 'HMS *Aurora* is a great product full of high quality detail, so much so, that it represents the best in this media I have built so far.'

Peter is a dazzle camouflage fan, and so sourced material from fellow modellers and Internet images to come up with an interesting colour pallet.

His seascape is artist's watercolour paper painted and varnished and then finished with AK acrylic water effects. His usual additional materials include brass rod cut to fit, Uschi van der Rossen rigging and stretched sprue for shorter runs.

He used superglue gel and pva as well as plastic cement. Painting was with Vallejo acrylics and then MIG weathering powders.

SCRATCH-BUILT *AJAX* 1:350 scale

By PHIL REEDER

This model is built mainly of plasticard and shows *Ajax* wearing the camouflage pattern as in early 1941.

HMS *Ajax*, mid-1940

Mountbatten Pink | White

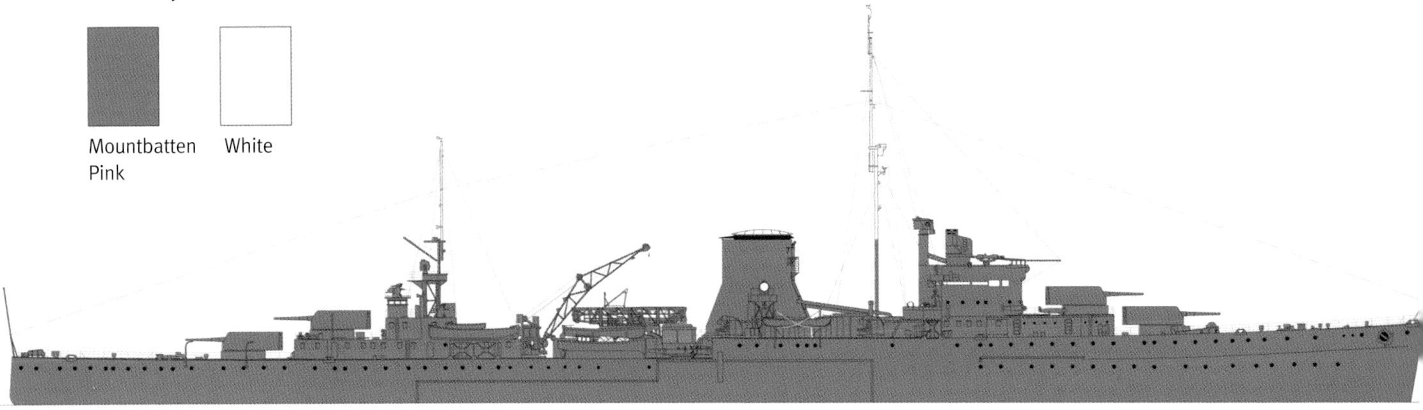

HMS *Ajax*, October 1942

MS2 | MS4A | B5

HMNZS *Leander*, 1942

507B | 507C

HMAS *Sydney*, 1941

507A 507C

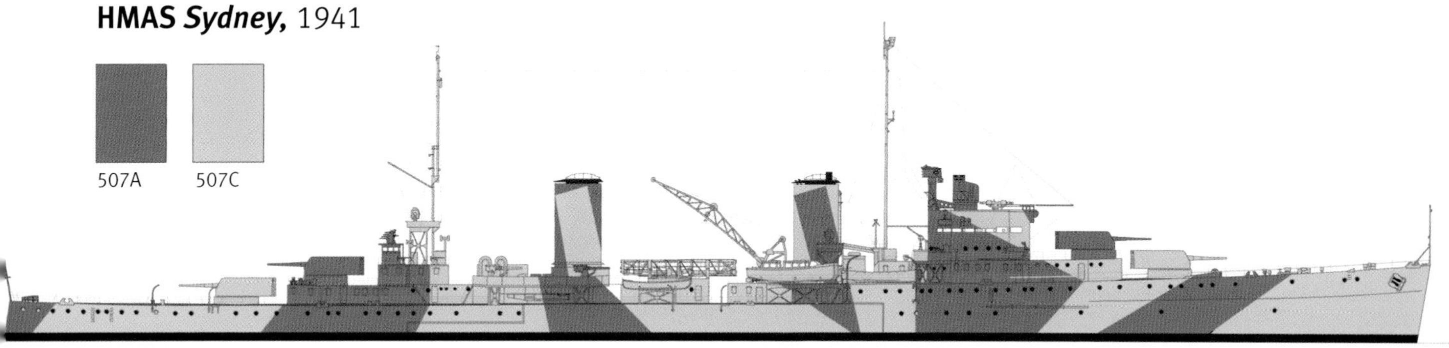

January 1941

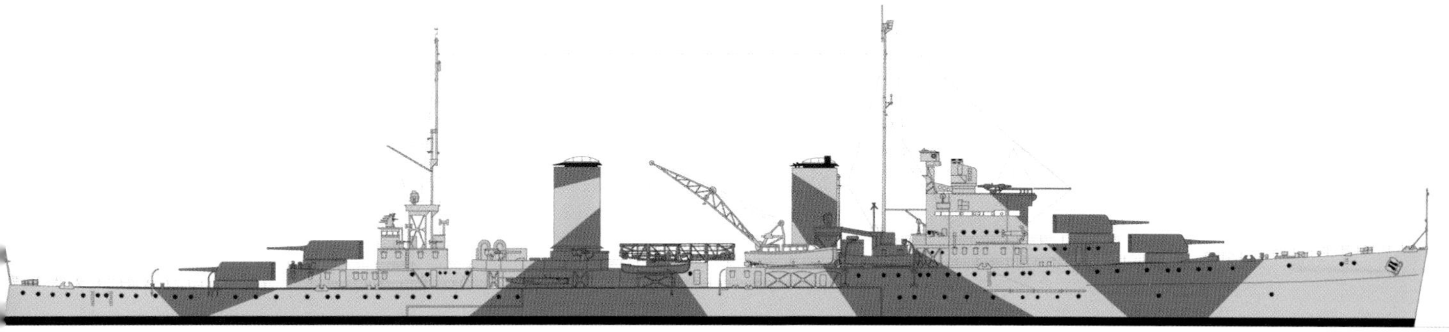

September 1941

HMAS *Perth*, 1942

507A

HMAS *Hobart*, 1944

US – 5N
Navy Blue

HMS *Arethusa*, 1942

HMS *Aurora*, 1945

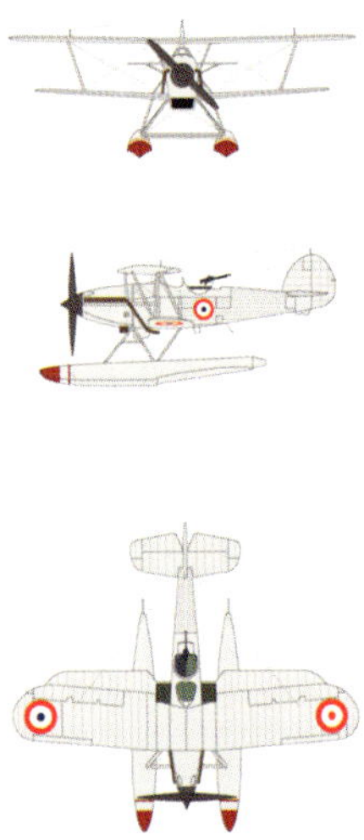

Hawker Osprey

Fairey Seafox

Supermarine Walrus

Camouflage

LEANDER CLASS

Leander

When *Leander* was serving with the Home Fleet during her early career, she was painted grey MS4A overall, with a scrubbed wood deck, only the bow area being painted dark grey. Whilst on loan to New Zealand, she was painted grey 507C overall.

In late 1940, she visited Alexandria where she received camouflage of light grey 507C with irregular straight-line patches of 507A. The pattern was the same on both sides and the need for regular repainting resulted in the exact pattern changing from time to time. One noticeable difference was that 'B' turret appeared in 507A in mid-1941. The decks were painted 507A.

On her return to New Zealand in late 1942, *Leander* retained the same camouflage scheme but the darker 507B replaced 507C. 'A' and 'X' turret tops were painted 507B and 'B' and 'Y', 507A. In early 1943, shortly after the aircraft facilities had been removed, *Leander* was painted dark blue overall, although the decks remained dark grey. In late 1945, *Leander* was painted G45 overall, with a hull panel in B15. After the war, she returned to grey MS4A with wooden decks.

Neptune

In her early career, *Neptune* was painted grey, either 507C or 507B, and carried neutrality stripes on 'B' turret when operating during the Spanish Civil War. Whilst at Alexandria in mid-1940, she received a dazzle camouflage scheme of patches of 507A, over 507C. The cruisers all had unique schemes, but *Neptune* had a mirror scheme on each side. In his journal, Midshipman Nigel Fawcett records her decks were painted blue. The pattern was amended slightly later in the year, becoming less angular, with wavy edges.

In early 1941, she received an Admiralty six-colour disruptive scheme using 507A, MS2, B5, B6 and MS4A. Turret roofs were painted 507C, except for 'B', which was B5. Decks were grey. The two sides were quite different. Later that year, to ease maintenance, she was painted in MS4A, with patches of B5 and B6 only. By the end of the year, the pattern was further simplified with MS4A (or 507C) and patches of 507A.

Orion

During her time on the American station, *Orion* was painted 507C, with wooden decks. Horizontal metal surfaces were darker grey, apart from the turret tops

Leander in pattern camouflage, photographed in Suva Harbour, Fiji, in February 1942. USS *Chicago* (CA-29) is in the background, at right. Note *Leander*'s radar Type SW on a lattice mast forward of the funnel, and the Supermarine Walrus aircraft on the catapult. *(US Naval History and Heritage Command, 0-G-7294)*

Orion photographed at Malta in October 1945 sports grey 507C with B20 hull panel. Note the 20mm guns on 'B' and 'X' turret and radar Type 273 on the aft superstructure.

Above: *Achilles* photographed in February 1942 carrying the Admiralty disruptive scheme. Note the radar Type SW on a lattice mast forward of the funnel, and the Supermarine Walrus aircraft on the catapult.

which were 507C. In 1940, she received a camouflage scheme, at Alexandria, of 507A and 507C. Decks were 507B.

In early 1942, *Orion* received a three-tone scheme of 507C, with areas of 507A and MS3. Decks were 507A. MS3 was not readily available in the Mediterranean, and so 507A replaced it when repainted. On D-Day, she had a MS2 hull and MS3 upperworks. In late 1945, *Orion* was painted 507C overall, with a B20 hull panel.

Achilles

As part of the New Zealand squadron, *Achilles* was painted 507C overall, with wooden decks. With the start of war, she was painted in darker 507B, but retained her wooden decks. Like *Neptune*, in early 1941, *Achilles* received an Admiralty disruptive scheme of MS4A with patches of B5, B6 and MS2. In mid-1942, *Achilles* sported a dark grey 507B hull and light grey MS4A upperworks. Decks were probably painted grey. After having 'X' turret removed, she was painted MS3, with a MS2 hull panel. The decks were grey.

Ajax

In her early days on the West Indian Station, *Ajax* was painted 507C, with a 'primrose' funnel and wooden decks. On the outbreak of war, she moved to the South American Station, changing to MS4A. On joining the Mediterranean Fleet Ajax was initially painted in Mountbatten Pink but from October to December 1940, she wore an unusual, unofficial scheme of 507C with areas of black and 507B. The funnel had black lines painted on it to disguise the shape.

In early 1941, whilst at Alexandria, *Ajax* had the areas of black enlarged, and outlined in dark grey. Later that year, she received a pattern of 507C with black disruptive dazzle areas. The next year, she was painted MS4A, with 'flowing' areas of MS2 and B6. Decks were mid-grey. The pattern had been only slightly modified by the time *Ajax* took part in the D-Day landings. Back in the Mediterranean, she was repainted in MS3, with a B15 hull panel.

MODIFIED *LEANDER* CLASS

Perth

Prior to transfer, HMS *Amphion* served on the South African station, with a white hull and grey upperworks, similar to 507B. As *Perth*, she was initially painted 507C overall, with wooden decks. The forecastle

Below, left: *Ajax* displaying the distinctive camouflage pattern painted in Alexandria.

Below, right: This profile view of *Perth* clearly shows both her camouflage and the rangefinder baffles fitted to the funnels. Note the Oerlikon mountings in zarebas on top of 'B' and 'X' turrets.

Above: *Ajax* shows the flowing lines of the camouflage pattern carried in October 1943.

and turret tops were painted 507A. In December 1940, whilst at Alexandria, she received a camouflage pattern of 507C, with flowing bands of 507A. Fifteen months later, she received a new pattern of the same colours, but which was less 'flowing' and included some straight edges. Steel decks were 507A, with turret tops matching the colour of the adjacent vertical surface.

Perth ended her career painted in grey 507A, which was badly worn due to a shortage of maintenance.

Sydney

Sydney was painted in the normal peacetime colour of 507C, with wooden decks. Horizontal metal decks were painted in a darker grey, but turret tops remained in 507C.

She obtained her first camouflage scheme whilst undergoing repairs at Alexandria in August 1940 – the usual 507C overpainted with areas of 507A, outlined for a while with 507B. The decks were stained blue. By the time of her return to Australia in early 1941, the shading had been removed and some changes made to the dark areas. Small changes to these dark areas were again made in March and September 1941.

Hobart

Before her transfer to become *Hobart*, HMS *Apollo* served on the West Indies Station, where her hull and superstructure were painted white and the funnels were painted buff. Her deck was scrubbed wood, with the forecastle painted grey 507B. At the beginning of the war, *Hobart* was painted grey 507C, but her decks remained as in peacetime. In early 1941 she was painted in darker grey 507A. The amidships decks stayed as wood, but the remainder were also painted 507A.

Below: *Hobart* photographed in November 1938, carries the red, white and blue 'neutrality' stripes on 'B' turret.

Hobart in July 1942, wearing her three-tone grey camouflage pattern. *(US Naval History and Heritage Command, 80-G-13454)*

In the middle of the year, *Hobart* received a camouflage pattern of 507A, 507B and 507C, but the decks remained as earlier in the year. In late 1941, the pattern was changed, eliminating 507B, but still using three greys, the mid-grey being an unusual mix. The wooden area of deck remained, but the rest was painted olive green with non-uniform black stripes.

After repair in New Zealand during 1942, *Hobart* received US Navy Measure 11 camouflage, with US deck blue. Before the end of the war, she was painted in US Measure 21, using dark blue 5/N. At the end of the war, *Hobart* went into reserve, painted as at the start of the war.

ARETHUSA CLASS

Arethusa

Arethusa was initially painted grey 507C, with wood decks. Metal decks were painted 507B, with forecastle 507A. She carried neutrality stripes on 'B' turret only. *Arethusa* was painted 507B overall on her return to Great Britain in early 1940. From the middle of 1940, whilst in the Mediterranean, she was painted 'Mountbatten pink'.

During April 1941, *Arethusa* received an unofficial camouflage scheme of 507C, overpainted in 507B, to make her appearance more suitable for operations in the Atlantic. Wooden decks were painted 507B. In early 1942, she received a four-colour scheme of MS4A, B5, MS4 and B15. Metal decks were 507A, and the wooden decks stained dark blue-grey, similar to PB10.

By the end of 1943, her hull, aft superstructure, fore funnel and 'A' and 'Y' turrets were painted G20, with the forward superstructure, 'B' turret and aft funnel in B55. The decks remained dark blue-grey, as previously. For the Normandy landings, *Arethusa* had her lower hull painted MS2, with the upper hull and superstructure in MS3.

In 1945, she was 507C overall, with a 507A hull panel. Once again, her decks remained dark blue-grey.

Galatea

Galatea started the war in the Mediterranean, where she wore the usual 507C with wooden decks, but on her return to Home Waters, she was painted 507A. In the middle of 1941, whilst in the Mediterranean, she wore 'Mountbatten Pink'. Later that year, *Galatea* received an unofficial pattern of 507C, with areas of 507A. Decks were wood, with 507B metal areas.

Penelope

Pre-war, *Penelope* wore the normal 507C, with wooden decks and 507C metal surfaces, except for 507A on the forecastle. She carried neutrality markings on 'B' turret. In 1940, while operating with the Home Fleet, she was painted white with areas of dark brown and dark green, to protect the ships while at anchor in Scapa Flow.

Penelope moved to the Mediterranean in

This starboard quarter view of *Arethusa*, taken in 1942, clearly shows the four-colour camouflage scheme. Also note the tripod masts, the aft HACS and the Oerlikon gun on top of 'Y' turret.

October 1941, and, according to Wright, was painted 'Mountbatten Pink'. This is not confirmed in other sources, and she had a dark grey hull with light grey upperworks when she joined Force 'K'. She received a major refit in New York Navy Yard in 1942, and on her return received an Admiralty standard scheme of MS4A, with disruptive areas of B5 and MS2. All horizontal surfaces were G10. In 1944, *Penelope* had a dark hull, 507A, with light upperworks, 507C. Decks remained dark grey.

Aurora

When first commissioned as a flagship, *Aurora* was painted in MS4A. Decks were wood, with MS4A metal areas, apart from right forward which was painted 507A. On joining the Home Fleet, all MS4a areas were repainted 507A. On moving to the Mediterranean in 1940, according to Wright, she received the usual 'Mountbatten Pink', but she is recorded as having a dark grey hull with light grey upperworks when she joined Force K.

During her repairs in the first half of 1942, *Aurora* received a four-colour disruptive pattern, comprising 507A, B5, MS4 and MS4A. Wood decks were stained grey, with horizontal metal surfaces painted in a similar colour. Turret tops were 507B, with the forecastle in 507A. The scheme was modified the following year but used the same colours.

In 1944, *Aurora* was MS3 overall, with a darker MS2 hull panel. Her tripod masts were painted white. Following a refit during the second half of 1945, she was repainted in 507C, with the hull panel in B20. The wooden decks were no longer stained, and the masts were painted black above the top of the funnels. She was repainted before going to Nationalist China.

Above: This photograph of *Arethusa* in late 1943 shows the two-tone scheme with the fore funnel and 'A' turret painted darker than the aft funnel.

Below: *Galatea* wearing a striking camouflage scheme in late 1941.

Bottom: The profile of *Penelope* in January 1944 clearly shows the camouflage scheme.

Modifications

LEANDER CLASS

The vessels were found to be wet amidships, and so the forecastle hull plating of all four cruisers was soon extended aft, level with the aft 4in gun.

Another common modification was the replacement of the four single 4in guns by twin mountings Mark XIX, with a maximum elevation of 80°. The forward mountings were repositioned further forward. The whalers to port and starboard, forward of the gun mounts, were moved aft, being positioned between the two twin mounts on each side. Apart from *Achilles*, which did not receive them until her 1943/44 refit, this was carried out in the 1930s. After sustaining damage to her boats, *Leander* had her plating extended aft to the fore 4in gun during a 1934 refit, when her boats were also repositioned. The 32ft cutters were stowed in davits on the forecastle deck, and the crutches under the 35ft motor boat and 36ft pinnace were raised to allow free flow of the water. The 30ft gig was temporarily stowed in the place allocated for a spare aircraft, which was never carried on any of the class.

A third common modification was the reinforcement of the pole masts with tripod legs to enable them to carry the heavier weight of the radar equipment installed.

Achilles and *Leander* were transferred on loan to New Zealand in 1936/37, and were fitted to operate the larger Seagull V or Supermarine Walrus amphibians. *Achilles* transferred to India in 1948, being renamed *Delhi*.

Leander

Leander received an aft fire control position during her 1936/37 refit, when her crane was also repositioned on the centreline. The crane had originally been offset for use with the Fairey IIIF aircraft, which proved unsuitable. The two quad 0.5in machine gun mounts on 'B' gun deck abreast the bridge, were moved to the aft superstructure.

Her catapult and aircraft were removed in June 1941, and replaced by a quadruple pom-pom mounting, but the catapult was returned later that year. It was removed permanently in 1943. Five single 20mm were added, including one atop 'B' turret and one atop 'X' turret. Radars were added in mid-1942 to the director and Type 291 at the masthead. A New Zealand Type SW air-warning radar was fitted between the bridge and the funnel on a tall lattice mast. In 1943 the aircraft fittings were finally landed and four single 20mm were fitted. Radar 273 was installed amidships. By April 1944 'X' turret had been landed, to be replaced by single 20mm (port and starboard) with a power-operated twin on the centreline. Two twin 40mm Bofors were fitted on the former motorboat platform, the remainder of the 20mm outfit consisting of two power-operated twins and two singles. The HACS on the bridge was replaced by two, port and

Orion in early 1942 shows the tripod masts, the extended hull sides and the twin 4in mountings. Note the splinter shields around these mountings.

HMNZS *Leander* on 25 July 1943 showing a darker colour scheme, with 20mm Oerlikon mounts on 'B' and 'X' turret, and on the quarterdeck. Note the freshly painted panel on the lower hull amidships appears darker as this colour was known to fade rapidly. The radar Type SW can be seen just forward of the funnel and Type 273 on the aft superstructure. The aircraft catapult has been removed, but she still has pole masts. *(US Naval History and Heritage Command, 80-G-56725)*

starboard on the lower signal deck. By 1946 all single 20mm had been landed and the quadruple pom-pom had been replaced by twin Mk V. Three single 40mm Mk III replaced the single and twin 20mm on 'X' gun deck.

Neptune

Neptune completed without her HACS or quad 0.5in mounts. The former was fitted quickly but she still lacked the machine gun mounts when undertaking patrol duties during the Spanish Civil War.

According to the ship's log, *Neptune* received her twin 4in guns in August 1938, but photographs show that her hull side was not extended at that time. She received a refit at Chatham from February to May 1941, when the forecastle hull sides were extended aft and splinter protection was added around the 4in guns. Radars Type 281, 284 and 285 were fitted on tripod masts, and a Vickers quadruple 0.5in gun mounting was added on 'B' turret, slightly offset to starboard and surrounded by a splinter screen.

The catapult was removed in July 1941, while *Neptune* was at Port Said, and a pom-pom mounting was fitted in its place. The ship's log records a second pom-pom being added in October 1941, probably sided on the catapult platform with the one fitted earlier in the year.

Orion

When *Orion* first had her single 4in guns replaced by twins, only two were available, and they were fitted in the after position. Her three quad 0.5in mounts were all situated on the aft superstructure.

Having been damaged in May 1941, she received temporary repairs at Simonstown

Orion photographed in 1942. Note the 20mm Oerlikon mounts on 'B' and 'X' turrets, on sponsons abreast the forward superstructure, and on the aft superstructure. Note also the tripod masts and the arrangement of the boats.

Achilles is shown after being handed over to India and renamed *Delhi*. 'X' turret has been removed and replaced by two twin 40mm mounts. Two more twin 40mm mounts have also been fitted abreast the position vacated by the catapult, now used for boat stowage. Two single 20mm Oerlikons have been fitted on each side, immediately forward of the two sided HACS directors.

in July/August, when her catapult was removed; *Orion* then underwent a major refit at Mare Island Navy Yard, USA, between September 1941 and February 1942. Two quadruple pom-poms were fitted amidships, abreast the position vacated by the catapult, which was now used for boat stowage. Single 20mm Oerlikons were fitted on the top of both 'B' and 'X' turrets, three mountings on the after superstructure, and two more in sponsons abreast the forward superstructure. Type 284 and 285 gunnery radars were fitted to the directors, and the two aerials of Type 279 were fitted at the mastheads.

Orion completed her 'As and As' in Great Britain in 1943, during which she was fitted with Type 273 radar, forward of the mainmast.

Achilles

Achilles landed all the single 4in and shipped ten 20mm guns in their stead in 1942, presumably as a temporary measure. One was fitted atop each of 'B' and 'X' turrets, and a pair fitted in lieu of each 4in mount. A New Zealand Type SW air-warning radar was fitted between the bridge and the funnel on a tall lattice mast, and the masts were strengthened by the introduction of tripod legs.

In 1943/44, the twin 4in mountings were fitted in lieu of the original single mounts, 'X' turret and the catapult were removed and four quadruple 2pdr were fitted, two in lieu of 'X' turret and two amidships. The 20mm now totalled eighteen, in seven power-operated twin and four single mountings. Two HACS were fitted on the lower signal deck, the bridge HACS having been supplanted by a radar aerial. In April 1945 the light AA consisted of four twin 40mm Bofors, two on the aft superstructure and two abreast the vacant catapult position; five 20mm twin Oerlikons, two on the quarterdeck, one on the top of 'Y' turret, and two on the main deck, abreast the bridge; and five single mountings, one on the platform aft of the mainmast, two on the aft superstructure abeam the mainmast, and two on the forward superstructure, abeam the bridge.

Ajax, photographed on 6 October 1943, whilst undergoing a refit in New York Navy Yard, identifying the new foundations for the light AA weapons and 44in searchlights, together with other modifications. Original key reads: (1) Fdtn. for 20mm twin mounts P/S.; (2) Fdtn. for 40mm quads P/S.; (3) Bbds. for 40mm R.S. Room P.S.; (4) Fdtns. for 44" searchlights.; (5) Modification of railing in way of gun mount.; (6) Brackets for FV1 reflectors.

Ajax

Gunnery trials on *Leander* caused slight blast damage on the bridge when 'B' gun fired at high elevation on extreme aft bearings. This was too late for modifications to the others, but *Ajax* had her compass platform projecting slightly forward, over the front of the bridge face.

After the Battle of the River Plate, *Ajax* received a refit which included the fitting of tripod masts, installation of splinter protection around the 4in mountings, and radar Type 279. She also received a heavier catapult and a Walrus aircraft in 1940.

In 1941 the catapult was removed and replaced by a quadruple 2pdr pom-pom. At that time she also carried three quadruple 0.5in machine guns, one on a platform aft of the mainmast, and two on the aft superstructure, abeam the mainmast. Six single 20mm were added early in 1942, two right aft on the quarterdeck, two on the superstructure just forward of the mainmast support legs, and two on the main deck abreast the bridge. Later the same year, the quadruple 2pdr on the catapult structure was landed, as were the 0.5in MGs. In their place the ship received two quadruple 2pdr on the boat platform, three more 20mm singles, two HACS on the lower signal deck and radars Type 272, 282 and 285. During a refit in the USA in late 1943, two quadruple 40mm Bofors were fitted in lieu of the quadruple 2pdr pom-poms, and four twin 20mm Oerlikons replaced four of the single mounts.

MODIFIED *LEANDER* CLASS

All had the fixed catapult replaced by a 53ft trainable one, in order to be able to operate the larger Seagull V or Supermarine Walrus aircraft.

Perth

Perth was refitted with twin 4in guns in lieu of the single mounts in 1938/39. Anti-range finder baffles were fitted to the funnels during a refit in Sydney in early 1940. A quad 2pdr pom-pom was fitted amidships in May 1941 at Alexandria but removed by July. Radar Type 286 was fitted on the mainmast at the same time, and the catapult removed and replaced by two 20mm Breda guns. A third was present on the quarterdeck for a short period, as was a quadruple pom-pom on the catapult deck, during the evacuation of Crete. Refitted at Sydney in late 1941, *Perth* had Oerlikons fitted on 'B' and 'X' turret. The two forward 0.5in mountings were relocated to the quarterdeck and replaced by Oerlikons.

Another photograph of *Ajax* in October 1943, whilst undergoing a refit in New York Navy Yard, showing 'A' turret. Note the carley float on the side.

In this photograph of *Perth*, the distinctive knuckle forward is clearly visible. Note that the twin 4in AA guns had been fitted by this time.

Sydney

Sydney received splinter shields for her 4in and 0.5in mounts, and possibly a few 20mm single mounts. Her single 4in guns were not replaced before she was lost.

Hobart

Hobart had her single 4in AA guns removed and replaced with twin 4in guns in 1938/39. Her catapult was removed when in the Mediterranean in June 1941 and replaced by a quadruple 2pdr pom-pom mounting, and two Italian Breda guns were fitted on the quarterdeck in December 1941. During a refit at Sydney from August 1943 to January 1945 following torpedo damage, the catapult structure was dismantled and two quadruple pom-poms installed abeam the aft funnel, tripod masts were fitted, the forward 4in guns repositioned athwart the forward funnel, and boat stowage was altered. Her single centreline DCT was replaced by two sided ones. Three twin 40mm Hazemeyer Mk IV and five single Mk III plus two quad 2pdr Mk VII mounts were fitted on the boat deck in September 1944. Type 281B air warning, 277 surface warning, 276 surface and close air warning radars had all been fitted by 1945, as had a SG surface warning set from America. Type 283 was fitted for main armament, Type 285 for the 4in mounts, and Type 282 for the 2pdr and 40mm mounts. Four twin 20mm mounts were landed, leaving just a single 20mm on 'X' turret.

In June 1946, 'X' turret was removed, to be replaced by Bofors Mk III and Mk VII mounts on the shelter deck.

ARETHUSA CLASS

Plating was extended amidships, in the entire class, to reduce wetness.

Arethusa

Arethusa received a HF/DF aerial at the head of her foremast early in the war, and by April 1941, had received two quadruple pom-poms amidships, and radar Type 286. She had also landed her catapult. Two UP mountings, one on quarterdeck and one on 'B' turret, and four single Oerlikons were added later that year. In September 1941, the single 4in guns were replaced by twins. By spring 1942, the UP mountings had been removed, and the quad 0.5in mounts replaced by four 20mm Oerlikons. During a refit at Chatham in early 1942, the Type 286 radar was landed and a Type 273 lantern fitted in front of bridge. Also, radar Type 281 was fitted at the masthead, Type 282 to control the quad pom-poms, Type 284 fitted on the main director and Type 285 on the HACS. The aft searchlight was moved to a position between the 4in guns and second HACS fitted. By October, three additional Oerlikons were fitted.

From March to December 1943, during a refit in the USA, the 2pdrs were replaced by quad 40mm Bofors, three single Oerlikons by twins, and radar modernised. By April 1944, the light AA comprised four power-operated twin 20mm and three single 20mm.

Galatea

Galatea had her catapult removed whilst under refit from October 1940 to January 1941. She also received two quad pom-poms amidships, eight Oerlikons (two between the twin 4in mountings, two forward of the aft funnel, and four forward of the fore funnel), and radar Type 279. Her single 4in guns were replaced by twins in December 1940.

Penelope

Penelope completed with twin 4in guns and a second HACS aft. Her catapult was removed, and she received two quad pom-poms and radar Type 281 at mastheads, Type 284 on the main director, and Type 285 on both HACS, during a refit from August

Hobart was torpedoed by a Japanese submarine on 20 July 1943 and so badly damaged that repairs lasted until January 1945. Seen here on completion of this work, she has gained two quad 2pdr pompoms amidships and the 20mm Oerlikons have been largely replaced and augmented by 40mm Bofors in single and twin mountings. A comprehensive suite of electronics included some US radar types, including a Mk 3 on the 6in director for surface fire control.

Left: In this overhead photograph of *Arethusa*, taken after her refit in the USA, the quad 40mm Bofors can be clearly seen on each beam.

Below: This view of *Penelope* in 1942 clearly shows the 20mm Oerlikon guns on 'Y' turret and the quarterdeck, and the 40mm guns either side of the tripod mainmast.

1940 to July 1941. Tripod masts were also installed. Four Oerlikons were added by the end of 1941, replacing two quad 0.5in mountings, and four more were added in the summer of 1942. A Type 273 radar lantern was fitted in front of the bridge.

Aurora

Aurora completed without aircraft facilities but with additional accommodation for service as Commodore (D). She also completed with twin 4in guns and provision for two HACS, which were fitted soon after. She received a UP mounting on the quarterdeck and two quad pom-poms amidships, during the summer of 1940. Radar Type 284 was added to the main director and Type 290 at the mastheads in April 1941. In early 1942, tripod masts were fitted, radar Type 281 replaced Type 290, Type 285 was added to HACS, and a Type 273 lantern fitted ahead of bridge. In August she received six Oerlikons and two quad 0.5in mountings. In 1944 single Oerlikons were fitted either side of fore funnel and bridge, and twin mounts on quarterdeck and 'Y' turret.

Above: A photograph of *Aurora* in December 1942, showing the 20mm Oerlikon gun on top of 'Y' turret.

Left: *Penelope* at Malta as she joined Force K in late 1941. She carries Type 281, 284 and 285 radars and quad pom-poms have been added, but she still carries the quad 0.5in mountings abreast the fore funnel.

HMS *Leander*, 1933

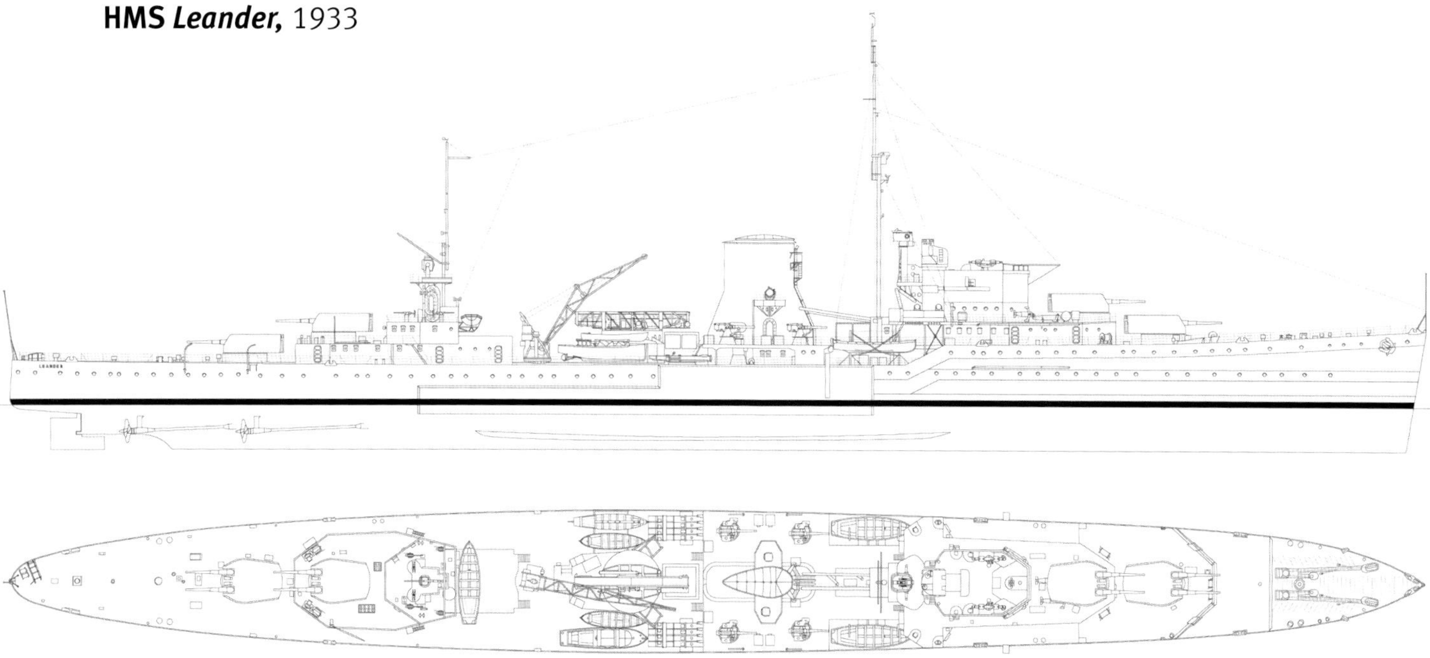

HMS *Ajax*, 1935, as built

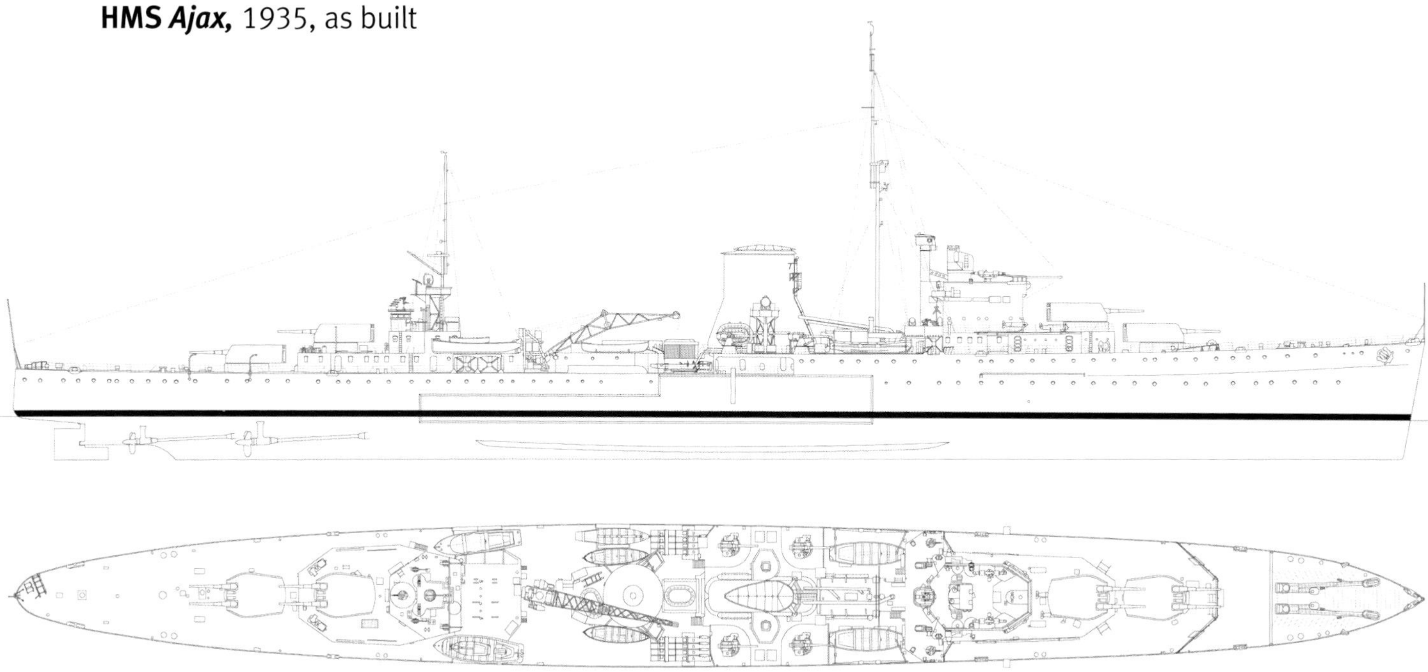

HMS *Ajax*, 1937

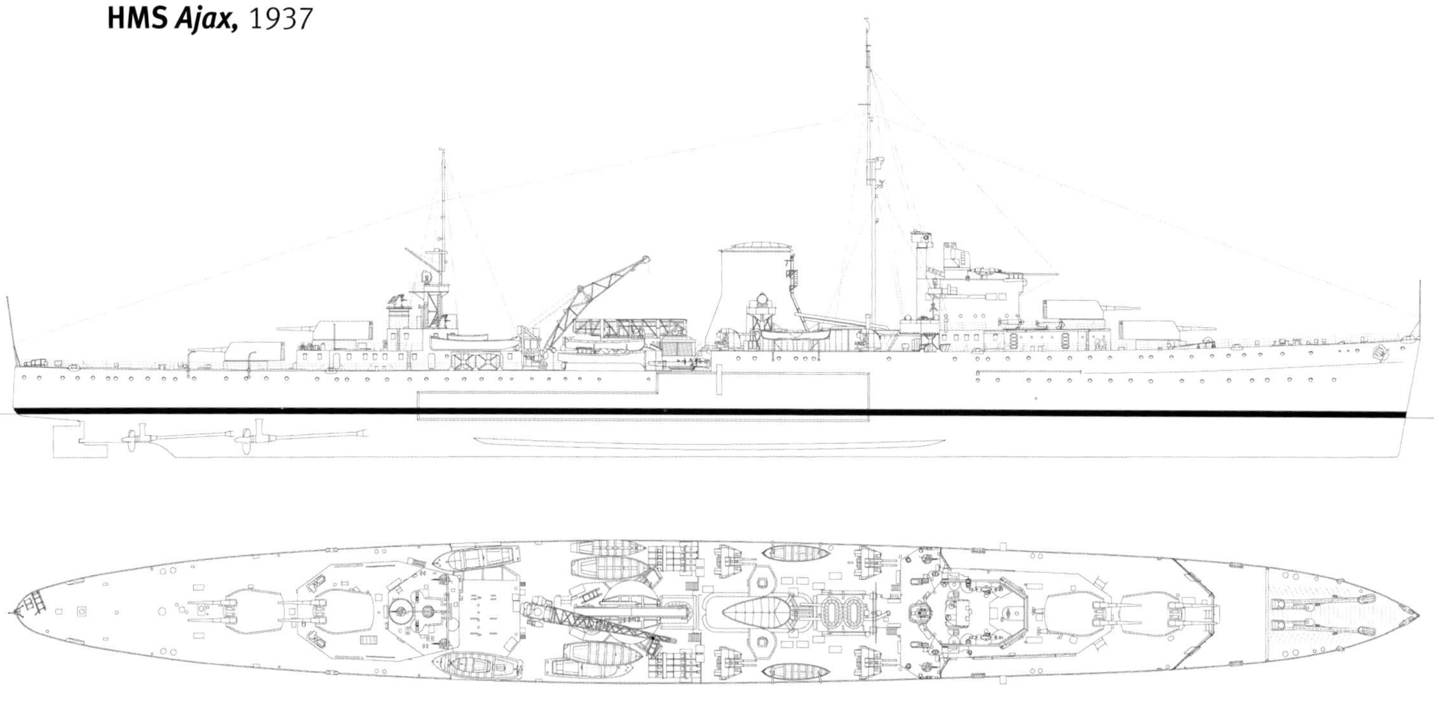

HMNZS *Leander,* 1942

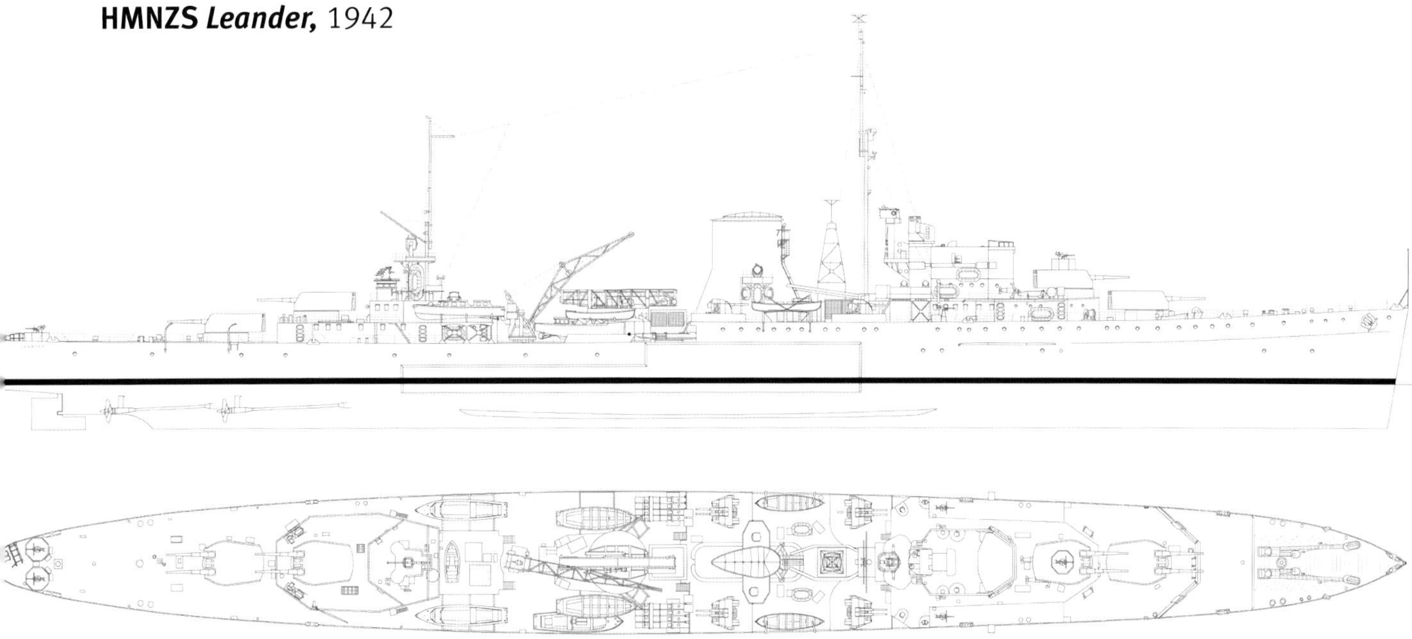

HMS *Ajax,* October 1942

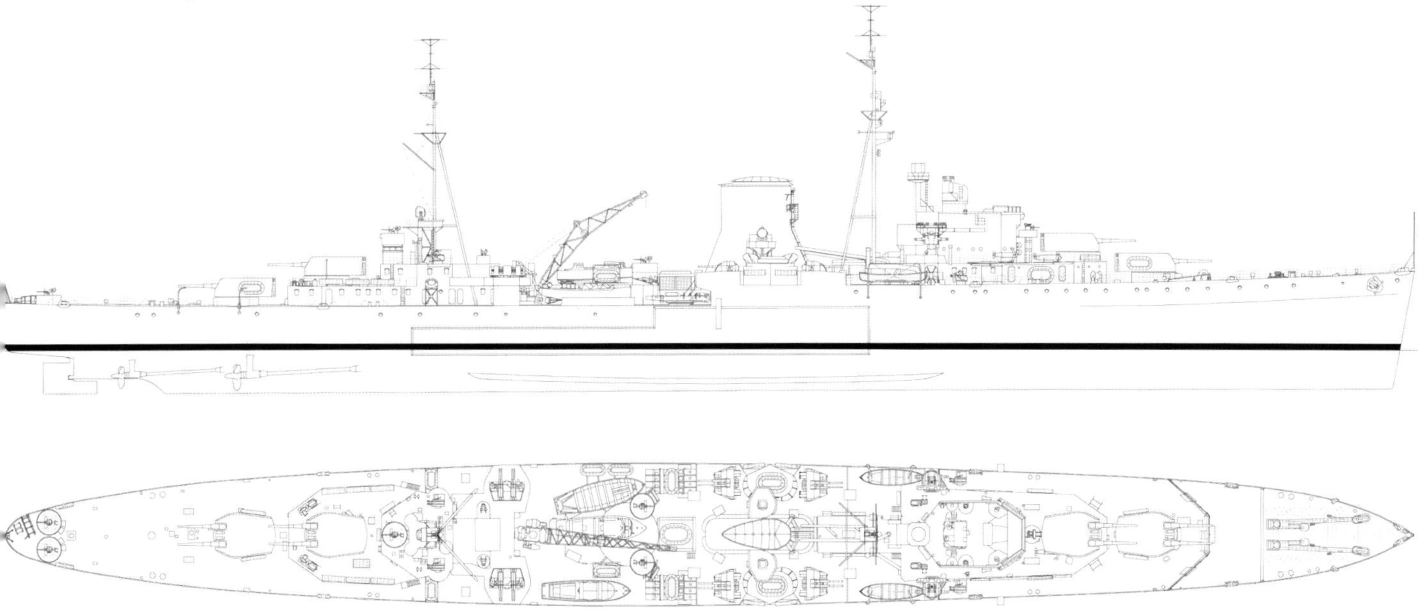

HMAS *Sydney,* 1935, as built

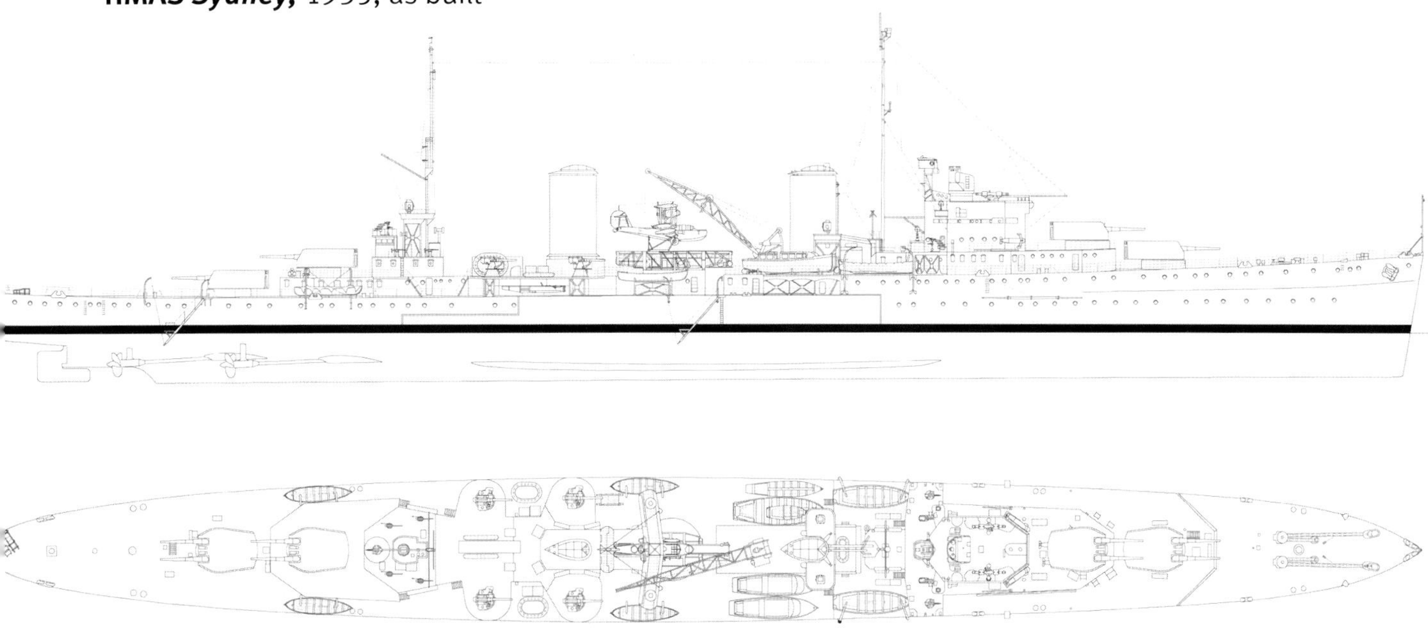

HMAS *Sydney*, 1941

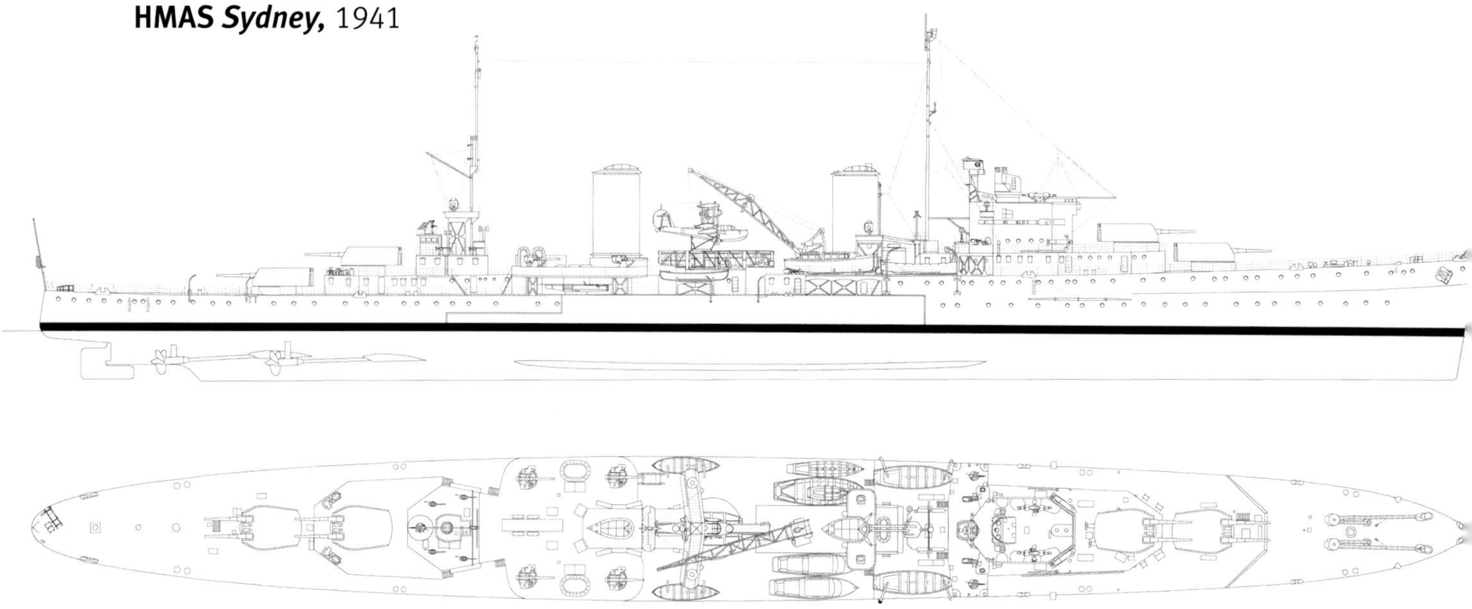

HMAS *Perth*, 1942

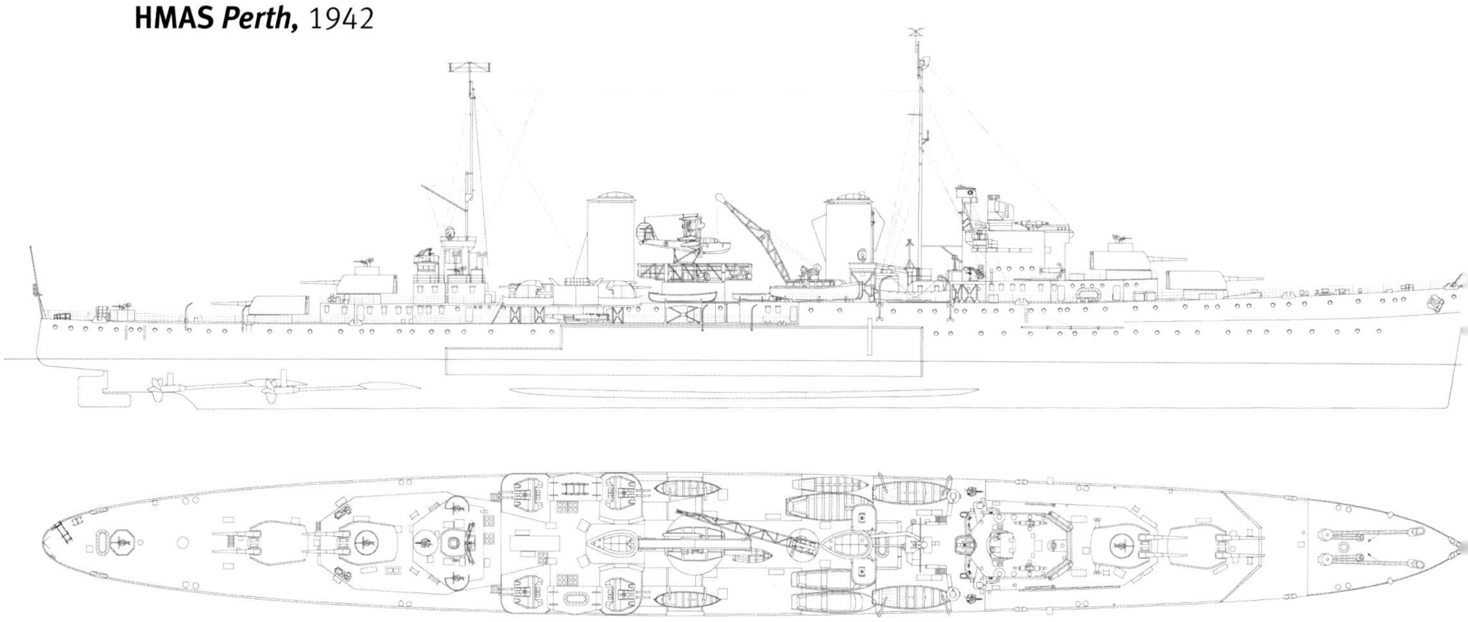

HMAS *Hobart*, 1945

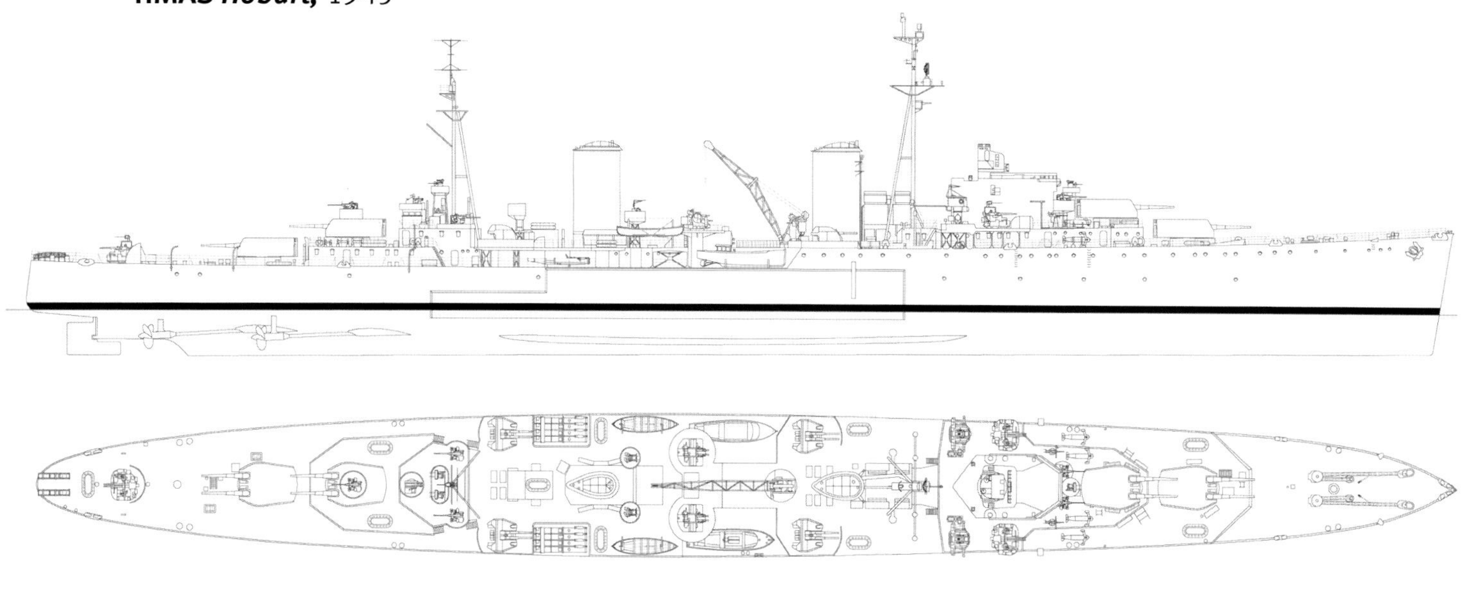

HMS *Arethusa,* 1937, as built

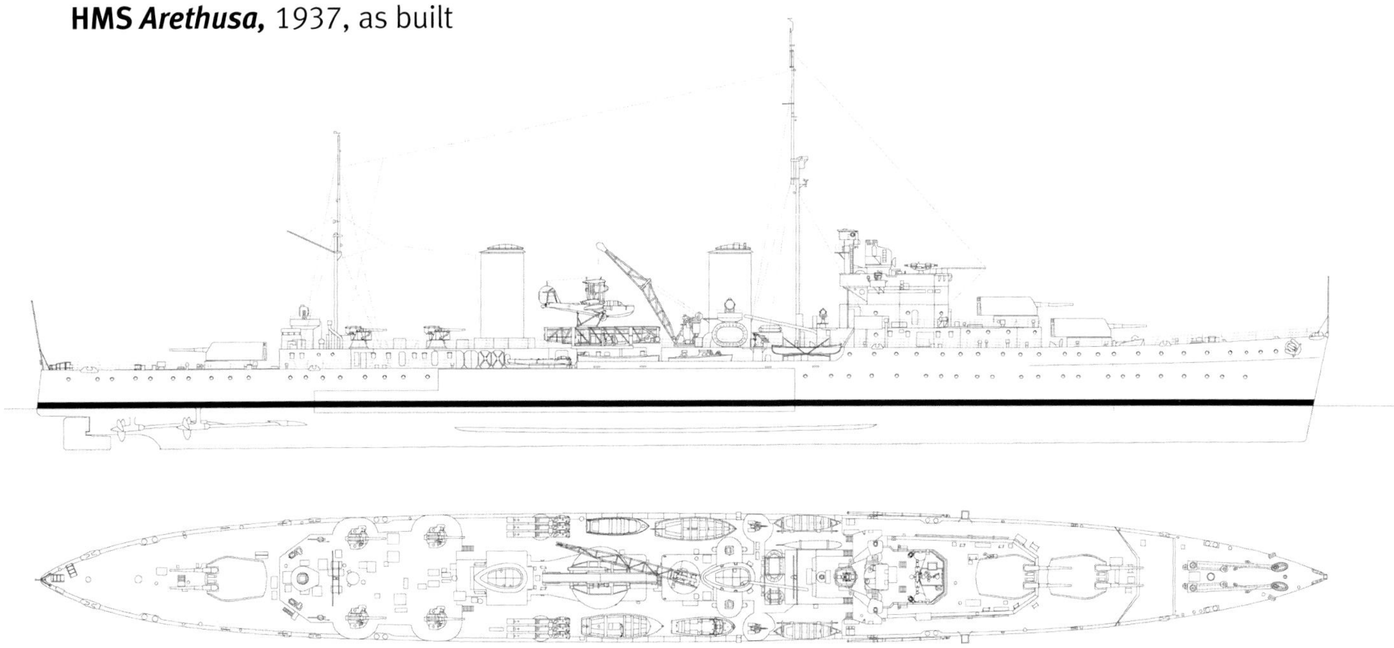

HMS *Arethusa,* 1941

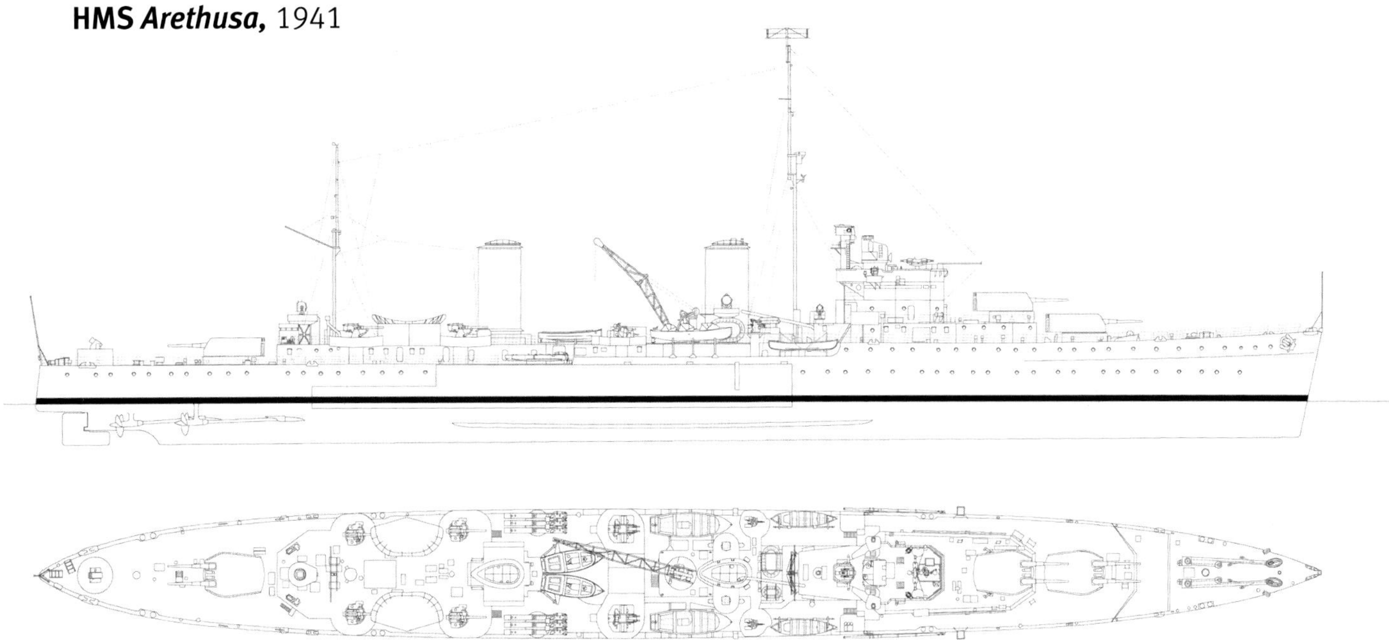

HMS *Aurora,* 1945

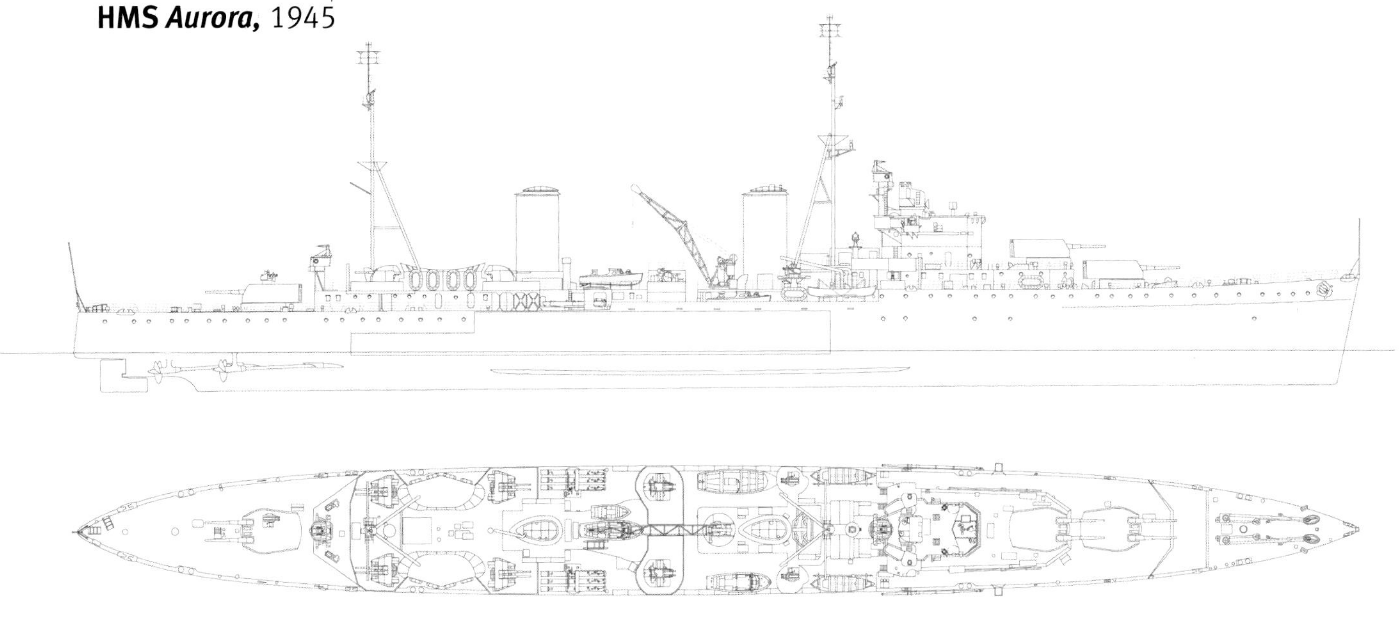

Selected References

BIBLIOGRAPHY

British and Commonwealth Warship Camouflage of WWII, Volume 3, by Malcolm Wright (Seaforth Publishing, 2016).

British Cruiser Warfare, by Alan Raven (Seaforth Publishing, 2019)

British Cruisers of World War Two, by Alan Raven and John Roberts (Arms and Armour Press, 1980).

British Cruisers: Two World Wars and After, by Norman Friedman (Seaforth Publishing, 2010)

British Warships of the Second World War, by John Roberts (Chatham Publishing, 2000)

Brytyjskie Krążowniki Typu Leander, by Zvonimir Freivogel (Okręty Świata 16, 2004). In Polish.

Conway's All the World's Fighting Ships, 1922–1946, edited by Robert Gardiner (Conway Maritime Press, 1980)

HMAS Perth, by Slawomir Brzeziński (Profile Morskie 66, 2004)

HMAS Sydney, by Slawomir Brzeziński (Profile Morskie 65, 2004)

HMS Ajax, by Slawomir Brzeziński (Profile Morskie 1, 2006)

HMS Neptune, by Slawomir Brzeziński (Profile Morskie 106, 2010).

HMS Neptune: Appearance, Camouflage and Armament, by Rorie Grieve, The Neptune Association (unpublished) at www.hmsneptune.com

Naval Weapons of World War Two, by John Campbell (Conway Maritime Press, 1985)

The Design and Construction of British Warships 1939–1945, Volume 1, edited by D K Brown (Conway Maritime Press, 1995)

The Modern Cruiser, by Robert C Stern (Seaforth Publishing, 2020)

Warships Perspectives – Royal Navy Camouflage, by Alan Raven (4 volumes, WR Press Inc, 2000–2003)

FURTHER READING

HMNZS Achilles, by Jack S Harker (Collins Publishers Ltd, 1980)

Well Done Leander, by Jack S Harker (Collins Publishers Ltd, 1971)

MODELLING WEBSITES

www.navis-neptun.de – German manufacturer of high-quality white metal models at 1:1250 scale.

https://nntmodell.com/en - German manufacturer of resin models at 1:700 scale, and a supplier of a wide range of kits by other manufacturers.

www.whiteensignmodels.com – US manufacturer of photo-etch sheets.

https://micromaster.co.nz – New Zealand manufacturer of 3D printed parts at many scales.

www.starling-models.co.uk – UK manufacturer of resin kits and etched brass detail sets, and supplier of a wide range of plastic and resin kits and accessories from international manufacturers.

https://www.atlanticmodels.net – UK manufacturer of resin kits and etched brass detail sets, including many kits previously produced by White Ensign Models (UK).

https://blackcatmodels.eu – French manufacturer of resin kits and 3D printed accessories.

www.tomsmodelworks.com – US manufacturer of photo-etch sheets.

www.larsenal.com – French manufacturer of resin kits and accessories.

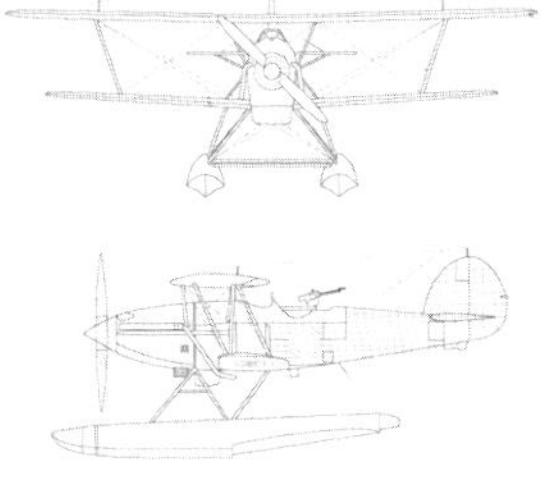

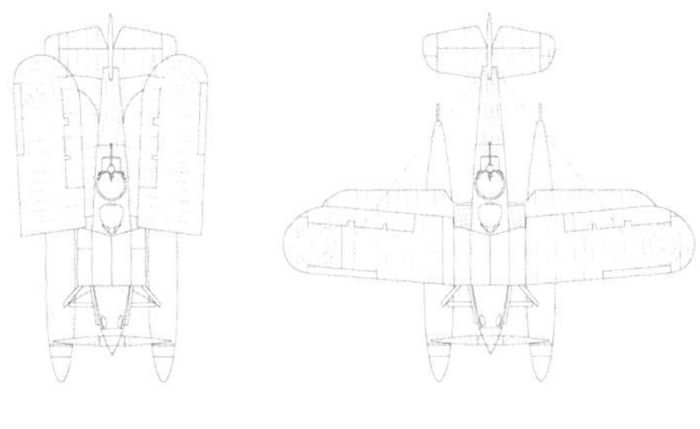

Hawker Osprey

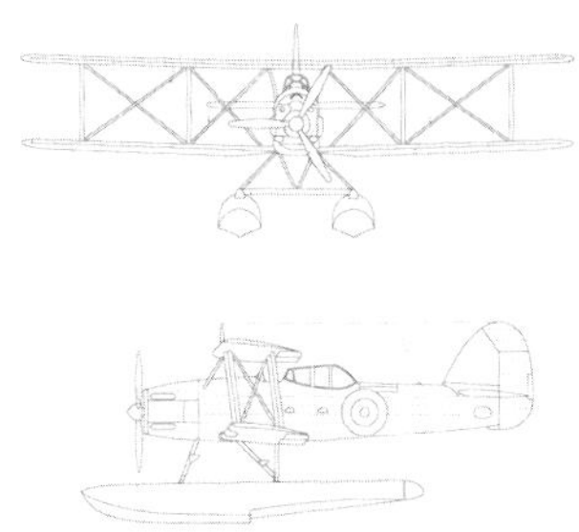

Fairey Seafox

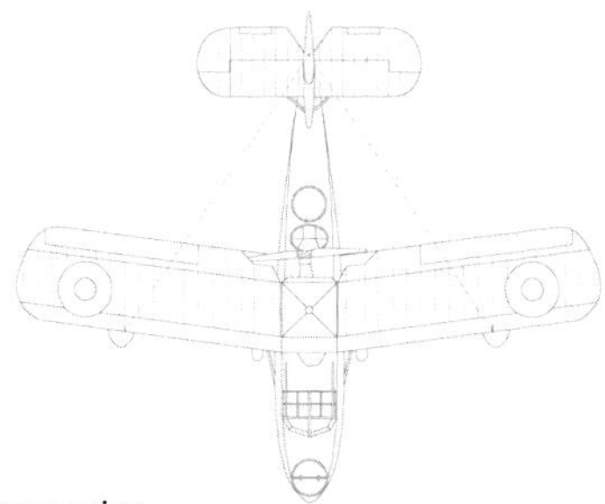

Supermarine Walrus

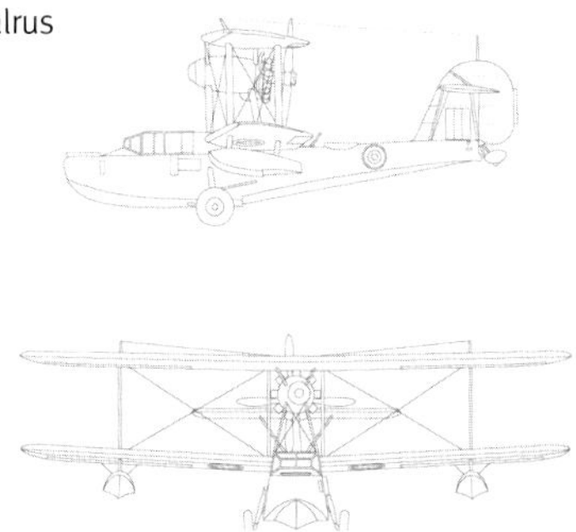